"In *The Magical Writing Grimoire*, Lisa Marie Basile leads readers into the limitless possibility of their own magick and healing through one of the most powerful modalities we have: the written word. Written with such poetess, grace, and honesty, this is more than a grimoire full of spells and prompts and rituals, but an offering to the self. Whether you're a witch or mystically inclined or not doesn't matter; words act as the thread connecting us all. This is a book you do not want to miss and one you should be sure to get for every word witch in your life."

—**Gabriela Herstik**, author of *Inner Witch* and *Bewitching the Elements*

"You don't need to consider yourself a writer or a witch to gain wisdom from what's inside this book. Using the strong framework found within her personal experience, Basile blends the art of ritual with inspiring explorations to aid you in pushing past creative, emotional, conceptual, and spiritual barriers. Truly a work of practical magic that's worth the journey!"

—**Laura Tempest Zakroff**, author of *Weave the Liminal* and *Sigil Witchery*

"If you love words, you love beauty, and you love looking deeply into the heart of things, this is the book for you. It will guide you on a spiraling journey of exploring your creativity, owning your power, and bringing about positive change in your life and in the world."

—**Tess Whitehurst**, author of *You Are Magical*

"This wonderfully detailed journal shows us that not only do we all possess great magic—witch or not—but it gives us the space to fully and shamelessly celebrate it. Get ready to be empowered!"

—**Amanda Lovelace**, author of *The Witch Doesn't Burn in This One*

"Words are powerful talismans. Lisa Marie Basile knows this. *The Magical Writing Grimoire* weaves personal stories with writing practices that will empower, heal, and inspire you. This beautiful book is one that you'll use again and again, whether you're a journaling fan, writer, witch, or just someone who is looking for a way to connect with spirit in an accessible, deep way."

—**Theresa Reed**, author of *The Tarot Coloring Book* and *Astrology for Real Life*

"Lisa Marie Basile's brilliant book guides you through the magic within the mundane act of writing. Her poetic style makes it a pleasure to read this book and her practical approach leaves you excited to start your own magical writing path."

—**Lidia Pradas**, author of *The Complete Grimoire* and blogger at *Wiccan Tips*

"Through numerous meditations, spells, rituals, and exercises, Lisa holds space to allow the reader to find their own voice as a force of personal truth, introspection, and manifestation. This beautiful book is sure to enrich a witch's relationship with their inner thoughts and words, enabling them to exert that into simple yet transformative magic."

—**Mat Auryn**, author of *Psychic Witch*

Inspiring | Educating | Creating | Entertaining

Brimming with creative inspiration, how-to projects, and useful information to enrich your everyday life, Quarto Knows is a favorite destination for those pursuing their interests and passions. Visit our site and dig deeper with our books into your area of interest: Quarto Creates, Quarto Cooks, Quarto Homes, Quarto Lives, Quarto Drives, Quarto Explores, Quarto Gifts, or Quarto Kids.

First Published in 2020 by Fair Winds Press, an imprint of The Quarto Group,
100 Cummings Center, Suite 265-D, Beverly, MA 01915, USA.
T (978) 282-9590 F (978) 283-2742 QuartoKnows.com

Fair Winds Press titles are also available at discount for retail, wholesale, promotional, and bulk purchase. For details, contact the Special Sales Manager by email at specialsales@quarto.com or by mail at The Quarto Group, Attn: Special Sales Manager, 100 Cummings Center, Suite 265-D, Beverly, MA 01915, USA.

24 23 22 21   3 4 5

ISBN: 978-1-59233-934-1

Digital edition published in 2020
eISBN: 978-1-63159-843-2

Library of Congress Cataloging-in-Publication Data

Basile, Lisa Marie, author.
Magical writing grimoire : use the word as your wand for magic,
  manifestation & ritual / Lisa Marie Basile.
ISBN 9781592339341 (hardcover) | ISBN 9781631598432 (ebook)
1. Grimoires. 2. Magic.
LCC BF1558 .B27 2020 (print) | LCC BF1558 (ebook) | DDC 133.4/3--dc23

LCCN 2019050160 (print) | LCCN 2019050161 (ebook)

Design and page layout: Tanya R Jacobson
Illustration: Ada Keesler, @adagracee, except pages 61 and 66 Lisa Marie Basile

Printed in China

The information in this book is for educational purposes only. It is not intended to replace the advice of a physician or medical practitioner.

The

MAGICAL
WRITING GRIMOIRE

*Use the Word as Your Wand for Magic,
Manifestation & Ritual*

LISA MARIE BASILE

" May I write words more naked
than flesh, stronger than bone,
more resilient than sinew,
sensitive than nerve. "

— SAPPHO

Contents

A Word of Welcome

INTRODUCTION

It's been said that "the tongue is a witch"—that is, according to George Webbe, an Anglican Minister in 1619 New England. And you know what? He was absolutely right. Every day we use our words to make magic and to transform ourselves and our communities. And no one can stop us.

Because, as anyone who has been pushed to the margins knows, language is at the heart of magic. Our words, full of intent and evolution, are our wands.

Anti-witch rhetoric has endured for centuries. In the 1600s, this so-called witch's tongue came from "wrongful" speaking—that is, daring to speak of anything that wasn't socially acceptable. Anything not clean and easy. Anything that didn't fall in line.

Of course, it was fear driving this rhetoric: If people (particularly women) spoke too boldly, too freely, or too truthfully, they might dismantle the shackles of society (or, you know, poison crops and kill men by way of a sideways glance).

This fear is still sadly relevant today. We watch marginalized groups fight against being silenced. Perhaps it has happened to you.

When we speak about our injustices, bodies, fantasies, magic, desires, sexualities, shadows, or mental illnesses, we are often seen as radical, crazy, or broken, proving that our words still hold immense power—when spoken digitally, on the page, or in a diary.

It is in feral response to that silencing—and in honor of our many diverse voices—that this book is born.

In these pages, you'll find a magic that is intuitive, elemental, shadowy, and spontaneous. It's a magic for nonlinear, imperfect, wild growth. The process is the focus; the magic happens when you devote time to ritual and to yourself.

Together, we will write our truths, our beauty, and our wildness while calling our shadows by their names. We will fully embrace the rebellion, power, and authenticity in the archetype of the witch, and we will conjure empathy, kindness, and power.

Language is magic. What we speak becomes, poems are spells, and you are a word witch.

CHAPTER 1
MAGICAL WRITING

An Introduction to
Word Witchery and
How to Use This Book

What is *The Magical Writing Grimoire*?

At the intersection of ritual and writing, *The Magical Writing Grimoire* is an exploration of the inherent magic of language (which I often refer to as "wordcraft" or "word witchery"). It encourages you to peek beyond the veil to where your voice lives. It is made for writers and non-writers, witches and non-witches alike. It was written to help us create better, more magical, and empowered lives.

The Magical Writing Grimoire is, of course, for writers and witches, but it is also for students, people working in dull day jobs, magic makers, creators, shadow workers, poets, therapists, educators, activists, the incarcerated, rebels, the lone freelancer, community leaders, group facilitators, the chronic illness and disability communities, sex workers, foster youth, the LGBTQIA community, and survivors.

Is Magical Writing for You?

Do you feel a glorious, ineffable otherness in your life? It's those things you can feel and intuit and dream—but cannot see or touch. Perhaps your hopes actualize in odd ways or your gut feelings are always right? Perhaps your dreams are somewhat prophetic?

Do you feel connected to air and stone, the sea and moonlight? Do you balk at the idea of chronic positivity and instead seek a magic of shadow and transformation? Do you connect with archetypes as inspiration? Do you connect with eclectic, intuitive, accessible magic—magic of your own?

Do you find yourself turning to books for comfort and breathing in the magic of old bookshops? Do you write poetry of magic and the body and nature? Do you keep a journal or grimoire—or perhaps want to start? Maybe you want to write spell-poems?

Perhaps you also come from a world, situation, or lineage of trauma or grief and you are looking for a way to both embrace and reconcile that pain. Or maybe you are seeking a tool or prompt for creating a more magical, intuitive, and intentional life—to heal, to celebrate your creativity, to honor your diversity, to resist, or to build empathy.

Maybe you just want a self-care tool that can be there through every tide. If so, your writing can be your lighthouse—whether you are a poet or diary-keeper or someone who loathes the sight of their own handwriting. This is not a book of judgement, rules, or traditional approaches to magic; rather, this is a guide written from one heart to another in an attempt to spread healing and autonomy.

Between these pages you'll find the crossroads of a magic born of poetics, self-exploration, archetypes, shadow work, nature, and everyday ritual. Here, the sacred and mundane collapse into one on the page. This is a magic for everyone.

If you read my book *Light Magic for Dark Times* (in which case, thank you, I love you!), this book goes deeper. But like that book, *The Magical Writing Grimoire* embraces poetry, accessibility, intersectionality, and healing.

The Magical Writing Grimoire is a love letter to the magic thread that connects our voice to the beautiful beyond. Throughout this book, what you read should be seen as a guide, not omnipotent text. It is important that you know that this experience is yours to modify, to make your own, and to translate into your own style and voice. I encourage you to do these exercises in whatever language you'd like, or in tandem with your own cultural or spiritual traditions.

" *Words themselves are means to emotional control over exterior phenomenon...* "

THE CRONE'S BOOK OF MAGICAL WORDS
BY VALERIE WORTH

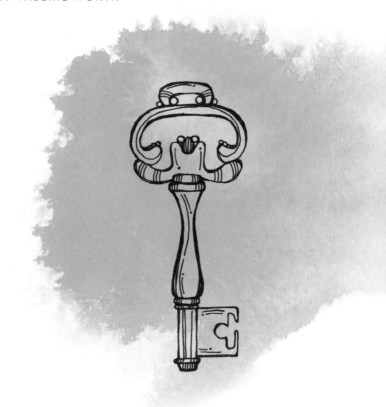

The Sacred Connection
Between Language & Magic

As a long-time poet and magic maker, word witchery, to me, is working with the inherent power of the word through art, poetry, diary-keeping, sigil creation, intentional journaling, and writing spells and rituals. Words are generative, as spells are, asking us to fall in love with the way they look, how they sing on and off the page, and how they feel in our bodies when we speak them out loud.

If magic is the manipulation of energy to create change, then writing is the ultimate magical act. With wordcraft, we can write our intentions into reality. From the stroke of the pen and the rhythmic chanting of the written word, from the blank page to the creation of word or story, we are using energy to generate both internal and external change.

Energy comes from intention (the most powerful tool you'll ever have), imagination, your breath, the elements, movement, sexual energy, and anything else you want to draw on. You can also call on the energy of elements, colors, crystals, archetypes, and more.

Instead of reciting spells written by others—archaic, sometimes gendered in ways we don't all connect with, or out of sync with our values—we can find empowerment by writing spells for ourselves. This is especially true if you have or seek a more eclectic practice.

When we begin to write for magical purposes consciously and intentionally, our bodies become an expression of our magic. Our hand's movements as we write are synonymous with wand waving. Our breath blooms into the stars.

Look at the etymology of the word *magic*, which has possible roots in the Old Persian *magush*. Magush means "to have power." The connection between the sacred and the scribe is woven throughout history as well. Consider the word *scriptura* (Latin for "writing"), which lent its meaning to the English "scripture," or religious text. Scriptures provide meaning and insight to readers, as well as a way to connect with or ponder divinity.

One of the root words for scripture is *skrībh-*, a Proto-Indo-European root meaning to cut, sift, or separate—especially in wood or clay. In this light, we can think of writing not only as how our ancestors communicated but also as an act of direct connection with and to the earth.

And then there's the well-known *Abracadabra*, which has been traced back to Hebrew as "I will create as I speak" and to Aramaic as "I create like the word." Again, the word itself builds worlds, casts a spell, sets a thing into motion. The word is at the center of all creation and plays a sacred role in many cultures.

The word "spell" itself, which is defined as "to tell" or "an utterance," became associated with magic in the Middle Ages, as if to speak something is to cause tangible change. As magic does.

In Ancient Egypt, Thoth was worshiped as the deity presiding over writing, magic, wisdom, and the moon. And then there's Seshat, an ally to the dead and the goddess of writing, libraries, books, and preservation. Seshat and Thoth's entangled associations with words and magic speak to the power of language and the written word.

For this reason, scribes were deeply respected in Ancient Egypt. It is said that they would habitually offer a single drop of their ink each and every day in Thoth's name. Ancient Egyptians also carried amulets inscribed with written spells, which would attract desires and manifest goals and intentions, or provide protection.

And of course, one of the most well-known phrases sanctifying the use of the spoken and the written word comes from the Bible's Gospel of John: "In the beginning was the Word, and the Word was with God, and the Word was God."

No matter what your belief, background, or practice, history tells us that our words have a transformative effect— and that's what we're here to harness, together.

Here's What You Can Expect from this Book

In your experience with *The Magical Writing Grimoire*, you will go on a written journey illuminated by guided meditations, journaling prompts, and accessible rituals—which largely focus on archetypes, the elements, and the shadow self—to bring gratitude, sustainability, authenticity, and power into your life.

You will be writing your own spells, investing in your deepest power, exploring the realm of personal ghosts, grounding in the present, and writing your desires into existence.

From trance journaling and letter writing for healing, to keeping a dream diary and moon-phase manifestation writing, you will find ways to use wordcraft as a tool to achieve self-care, hope, resistance, and intention in your life. You may already be using writing in your practice; in that case, this book embraces and explores that part of your routine.

You'll find:

- poetic and magical musings
- guided journaling and meditation prompts
- rituals for healing, manifestation, creativity, and more
- notes on the intersection of witchery and word
- moon phase, candle, sigil, astrological, dream, crystal, and other practices
- tools for writing your own spells
- peeks into my own magical writings and poems
- ways to write kindness, love, support, and inclusivity for others

The Inspiration Behind this Book

One bright summer morning, my grandfather, just sixty-three, brought me to the kitchen table, where he'd set out a calligraphy writing set. I was seven. Months later, he'd die from emphysema—contracted from working with asbestos after his time in the Navy.

But on that summer day, he wanted to connect with me, his only grandchild. He knew he was dying. So we sat together at the table drawing cursive letters onto large, white sheets of paper, and I felt as though writing was the most powerful thing he could have given me.

Though my grandfather's love for me was bright and real, he was also a complicated man, someone that cast a shadow on my family in his own ways. Substance abuse was rampant in my family, and although he had become healthier later in life, the damage had been done, to some extent anyway.

By the time he died, he was a changed man—yet the trauma still lived on. Through blood. Through stories. So, even as a child, I began to understand that writing could help me sort through the complexities of life—things like ancestral trauma and complicated grief and forgiveness and healing.

Today, I often fall into the abyss of nostalgia, wondering how my grandfather could have known that what he'd given me would stay with me in perpetuity. Why calligraphy? Why writing? It remains a mystery I'll never solve. I like to think it was a parting ritual, in some sense, his showing me how to create those magnificent letters. He left me with a newfound capacity to express myself, to immortalize the everyday, and to heal.

Even as a child I created secret alphabets and wrote wishes on paper, sending them down the town river to manifest. I buried letters I'd written about my parents—how they had hurt me or what I wish I could tell them—in soil.

If it weren't for the power of words, I wouldn't be here right now, and that's largely because it got me through some of my darkest moments in life.

I am still working through the trauma of instability and loss of childhood that took place during my formative years. And this book is a product of that process.

Abandonment issues, deep-rooted shame, resistance to change, familial and ancestral trauma, extreme fear, need for validation, anxiety and sadness, problems with trust; these are some of the issues writing and ritualized writing has helped me work through.

So I wrote this book from a few core perspectives: As a poet, writer, and editor; as someone recovering from chronic PTSD; as a former foster youth; as someone who lives with a chronic illness and advocates for awareness around it; and as a magic maker and shadow worker.

Over the years, I've turned to writing to deal with grief, trauma, and all sorts of tricky topics, many of which I've written about in magazines or in my books of poetry. It is my language of healing.

If you can't tell, I don't come from a structured background, so I tend toward the unstructured. Because of this, I'm very eclectic in my magical practices. I tend to go with the intuitive and chaotic, preferring to write my own spells, often off-the-cuff, than use someone else's. I am also a big proponent of shadow work as a core element in my practice—which is why it's a major thread in this book.

Shadow work, or the process of exploring your "disowned self," allows you to make magic from the parts of yourself that you repress or refuse to nourish because, sometimes, it hurts too much.

As Taisia Kitaiskaia and Katy Horan write in *Literary Witches: A Celebration of Magical Women Writers*, "Witches and women writers alike dwell in creativity, mystery, and other worlds. They aren't afraid to be alone in the woods of their imaginations, or to live in huts of their own making. They're not afraid of the dark."

I was never afraid of the dark because I believe there is always a light somewhere, even if you have to write it into existence.

The Magical Writing Grimoire also has roots in a 2018 writing ritual workshop I hosted at the splendid HausWitch in Salem, Massachusetts, a writing magic workshop I led at Manhattanville College in 2019, and a piece I wrote about poems as spells for Brooklyn-based bookstore Catland Book's *Venefica Magazine*. It has been, in short, a long time coming.

Of course, my work for *Luna Luna Magazine*, which I founded seven years ago, started it all. I began publishing rituals and writing prompts online around 2013, and connecting with readers about their love for ritual and writing made me voracious for further exploration.

Luna Luna Magazine is built on a foundation of intersectional feminism, shadow exploration, magic, the witch as an archetype, and art. It explores the duality of light and dark, and honors both as one.

I started *Luna Luna* when I began sensing my own magic. In truth, I'd felt the "shift" happen, like seismic quivers, years before then. It was gradual and soft. Before this point, I'd quieted my intuition, stifled my teenaged interests in the occult, and let my traumas harden me. I felt spirituality was something that only "better" people could have.

But slowly, I began tasting the fruit of the mystery. It was sweet and ripe, growing like vines throughout my life. Magic was happening in my written work.

Most of my traumatic feelings came out in my own poems, but providing a space via *Luna Luna* for others to explore their darkness also showed me the power of the written word. And then one day, I wrote an essay on my foster care experience for the *Huffington Post*. It was the first time I'd publicly mentioned it. Ever.

The moment this piece was published a spell was cast: This gesture de-stigmatized my experiences. I was taking ownership of my pain, releasing myself from its haunting grip.

But it didn't matter if my story was published or not. What mattered was that I was honest enough with myself to write it, to get it out of me and onto a page. I started ritualizing my writing space around this time. I'd light candles and write near symbolic objects. It was my way of feeling empowered and honoring the sanctity of my words.

It also took meeting witches and secular people who embraced the archetype of the witch to understand that pain, trauma, and a person's authentic, flawed self are all welcome in a witch's house.

It is a home where nature teaches us, where the feral self is celebrated, where healing is nonlinear, where the shadow is embraced, and where power is built—even from rubble.

When we strip away the need to fit in, or appear "okay"—in physical, mental, cognitive, or emotional ways—we become powerful in our vulnerability. It is in this state that we grow and bloom. It is in this state that we encourage others to join us. It is in this state that we embrace magic. Writing allows us to feel and be that.

From the many witches and writers I interviewed before starting this book, it seems many of us feel the need to reclaim our stories and share our voice—with others, with the cosmos, and with ourselves.

What this Book Isn't

While this book can be used to support a magical practice, trauma recovery, and self growth, it is not meant to replace traditional psychological care, nor is it an instructional book on witchcraft, Wicca, or any specific magical path. There are many other books that can do that for you—and some are included in the resources section at the end of this book.

This is a book that offers an approach to magic and ritual, one that can be adapted, expanded upon, and used to augment your own practice. It makes no claim to know or offer all the answers. In essence, this is a book of questions.

Must You Be a Witch to Use this Book?

Absolutely not. *The Magical Writing Grimoire* can be used by anyone—including atheists, practiced witches, the spiritual, or the religious.

Within these pages, we will honor and embrace the archetype of the witch as a symbol of power in the face of oppression, blame, and shame. We will explore the witch as a natural being. As a dreamer. A creator. A lover of darkness and light. Of righteous anger and deep empathy and everything in between.

As Kristen Sollée writes in her book, *Witches, Sluts, Feminists: Conjuring The Sex Positive*, the witch has been defined as an evil sorceress and an ugly, aging hag—just as she's been defined as a sexy, beguiling, femme fatale. She can't catch a break—so why not reclaim the word?

Through writing, and through ritual, we create a space for ourselves to share our voice and exist as ourselves. We reclaim our identities and narratives. If you identify as a witch, you're welcome here. If you don't, you will still find magic here.

How to Use this Book

The Magical Writing Grimoire is a companion to anyone who wants to explore the intersection of journaling, poetry, ritual, and intention. This book necessitates a deep dive into the abyss of the self, and its goal is to help you reclaim the story of your life and create sacredness from a blank page. It is designed to be accessible and adaptable, but it requires real work. Wordcraft isn't a fuck-around type of magic.

Unattached to any specific tradition, belief system, or magical path, *The Magical Writing Grimoire* leans into magic and the archetype of the witch but is wide open enough for you to explore, adapt, and challenge its words.

As Astrea Taylor writes in *Intuitive Witchcraft*, "Although the intuitive path could appear to be aimless to some, it's because we're following our hearts in the dark, guided by the small but steady inner voice of our intuition."

To use this book, you'll want to find a dedicated journal, something that feels comfortable and authentic. Of course, you're more than welcome to use any assistive devices (perhaps you like to speak into a recorder or type onto a computer because writing hurts your hands).

You will use this journal—which I call a *grimoire poetica*—for a great deal of what's in this book, including the journaling prompts and rituals, and much more.

You won't need to use the book in a linear fashion (and I hope you don't!). Three chapters focus on specific, magical writing-focused rituals—including manifestation, mindfulness, and healing—while the last chapter provides open-ended writing prompts. Writing is at the core of this book, and whether you engage in ritual or simply free-write, everything here is designed to inspire your exploration and creativity.

I recommend that you open to the pages that call out to you. Resist the linear! Chapter 2, however, does serve as an introduction to the core ideas within this book, and it also offers some specific writing techniques for you to incorporate as you move through the book.

Some of the writing exercises in this book will require you to enter a meditative or trance state from which to write, elevating you from the physical to the divine. I recommend you do these when you have time, space, and privacy.

Although writing is the foundation of this book, you will also come across rituals and prompts that hone in on archetypes, elements, shadow work, and intuition.

When we work with archetypes, we'll be working with an idea that has long been used in magical workings. Archetypes are ideas and symbols, or, in psychiatrist Carl Jung's words, they are "the formulated meaning of a primordial image by which it was represented symbolically."

The archetype of the witch anchors this book. The witch is a symbol of power: the feral, the sexual, the unapologetic. The witch is the being within us who blooms outside the constraints of social order, who seeks agency, resistance, progress, personal change, and healing. Archetypes could include the witch, the saint, or the femme fatale. An archetype might even include your unbridled self—a self we will write about and explore in ritual.

Beyond working with archetypes, we'll be working with the elements: fire, water, wind, and air. These four elements are a source of power in our magical practice as much as they are symbolic of the unique energies we have within us—or that we'd like to tap into. Throughout this book, you'll be calling on the elements as symbols of the self: like the water's depth and the earth's stability. These will come up in our writing exercises and in our rituals.

As you move through this book, you will unearth a specific part of your hidden self—the shadow. The shadow is where we keep those obscure feelings, the things we tuck away, the secrets we refuse to confront, the confessions we speak nothing of, the fears and traumas that haunt us. The shadow is neither good nor bad; it is part of the whole, and it functions as an abyss that can help us either heal or hurt. When we confront (and write about and to) our shadows, which we will be doing throughout this book, we make room for the light.

Regardless of what we do— whichever practice, ritual, or spell we cast or write—we'll be following the principle of intuition. What we feel in our gut is the most important aspect of our magic; it is what witches try to develop throughout their lives, and it is what you should pay attention to as we move through the book. If a poem, sentence, spell, or ritual component doesn't feel right, change it. Adapt, translate,

or update it to fit your needs, emotional capacities, or culture.

Lastly, this book honors accessibility; where possible, I will provide alternatives to certain ritual acts (a bath may be swapped for hand washing; dance may be done sitting or swapped for another act; writing by hand might be swapped for using an interpretive device), but I encourage you to go with what feels right.

I'll also include materials that are symbolic and useful, but that may be swapped for others. I do not believe that expensive or hard-to-access items are the only way to develop a spiritual or ritual practice. The world already caters to the privileged when it comes to self-care and therapy; while this book should not be used in place of medical care, it is meant to be an accessible and friendly source of support for everyone—especially those who don't have access to help. The only thing you'll truly need is a journal (or a computer).

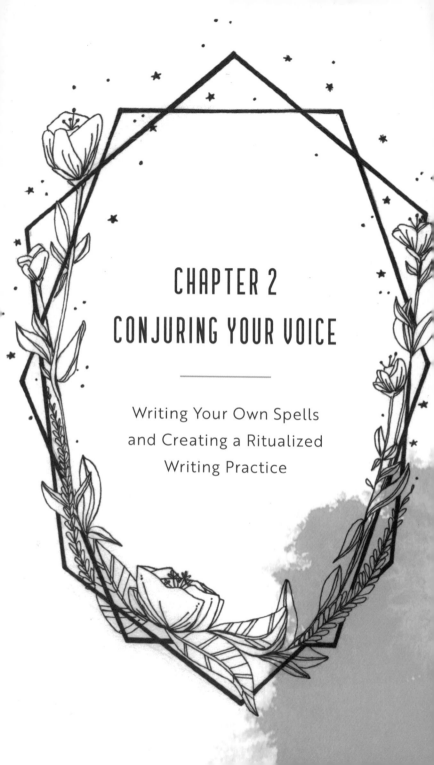

CHAPTER 2
CONJURING YOUR VOICE

Writing Your Own Spells
and Creating a Ritualized
Writing Practice

You stand within a space of mirrors. Below you, the floor is sand. Above you, a great expanse of sky. The gold and blue mix, speak, fall as one into their reflections. You are cradled by the earth and the sky. You realize that you are the reflection of the earth, that in all things you are found. And all things are found in you. Words, etched into the sand, guide your way as you move. They read, "create your own path." Walk through the mirrors, following the path, feeling your way through the maze, separating where the sky meets your body and where the earth joins your skin. When you see yourself as part of nature, what do you learn? Do you intuit your way through the maze? You realize that your power comes not from finding your way back into reality but by wading through the mystery, exploring the union of your body and nature. How do you create your own path through the labyrinth? Do you let the sky guide you? Do you ground yourself in the earth rather than follow the reflections?

Do you find fear or freedom in the autonomy of creating your own way? What words rise to the surface as you move through this space? Which words reveal themselves to you?

The Power of Ritual

In this chapter, we'll explore the beauty of ritual, creating a sacred space, and writing your own spells. We'll also look into a few writing methods that you can turn to within rituals in the pages ahead—or in your own craft and journaling practice.

But why would you *want* to practice ritual—especially a writing ritual? What could possess us to wade through the abyss of our secrets and fears and traumas? Would that not bring up pain or trauma—rather than dissipate it?

Writing our selves and our narratives and our dreams—with all of the shadows and beauty that come with it—is a form of reclamation. Our words give us autonomy and direction. Our words are our wands.

And if our magic is found in the ways we live our lives, treat others and nature, and affect change for ourselves and at the community level, then writing and writing ritual enable us to direct that magic in specific, unique, and organic ways. Simply put, writing is transformative. It is a freedom that many of us are privileged to have; it is a freedom that yields transformative results.

People have long turned to ritual for comfort, release, and manifestation. Ritual helps us take back control, direct energy for change, and heighten or color in our experience of being alive. Put simply, ritual is something we *do* as well as a *space* we inhabit; in ritual we are connected to ourselves, our personal truths, and greater truths.

When it comes to healing, studies have found that ritual and ceremony can be therapeutic, especially in cases of post-traumatic stress disorder or in the chronically stressed. That's probably something many of us can relate to.

A review in the *Journal of Traumatic Stress* found that ritual helps us, "contain intense emotions . . . compartmentalize the review of the trauma [and] provide symbolic enactments of transformation . . ."

The review also found that common rituals of healing include elements of forgiveness and release. Of course, other rituals involve hexing, binding, and rewriting of personal narrative. You won't find judgement here. Plenty of cultures and practitioners and paths encounter healing magic differently. Here, we'll use writing.

Whether from poverty, politics, sexism, transphobia, racism, fat-phobia, illness, social isolation, grief or anything else, trauma and stress cause our bodies and minds to become deeply taxed over time. It can hurt simply to be alive, and often it feels like we are on the brink of wilt, that we are alone in the muck, lacking autonomy and a path.

In short, ritual (and our magical writing practices within and apart from it) is going to look different to everyone; it is amorphous and beautiful and unique to the practitioner.

In this chapter, you will begin your journey by finding rituals that will introduce you to the power of writing ritual and spell-writing. They are designed to help you explore the DNA of this book: archetypes, nature, intuition, accessibility, and the shadow.

When we engage in writing rituals, we hone and direct our true energies into the word, tapping into a natural and intrinsic tool—self-expression. This gives us a chance to both experience energy and manipulate it to our will.

To make change through magic, we must first have a clear vision. We then must direct that energy clearly so that the vision is actualized. Ritual and ritualistic writing provide a personalized framework for this. Words allow us to give shape and meaning to our magic and to carry it with us wherever we go.

We can't always carry a candle in our pocket, but we can carry written spells or sigils, and we can write wherever we are.

When I began using writing as part of my ritual life, I discovered that I could take what felt abstract, the small beads of emotion rolling around within my mind—my thoughts, my feelings, my desires—and create something physical, living. Writing always helped me bridge that gap, and so this chapter focuses on learning how to integrate writing rituals into your life and why they are important.

What words come to mind when you tap into your own light, and what is the story of your dark?

" *We travel, some of us forever, to seek other states, other lives, other souls.* "

— ANAÏS NIN

Integrating Wordcraft & Ritual into the Everyday

Ritual, a sacred act, is a sustained dedication to something: healing, energy-raising, casting something out, manifestation. In this book, you'll create rituals around your writing and integrate writing into your rituals. It's all one.

First, you'll need to make time for ritual and writing.

Maybe you stretch every morning or you meditate before you write. Perhaps you enter a trance state as you write. Ritual is a repetitive process that influences our bodies and minds; in doing so, we are wiring ourselves into ritual. And that energy attracts change.

Begin this chapter by choosing a day or more each week or even an hour each day to dedicate to ritualized writing. Maybe you choose a weekend or a week night,

but whenever you choose, make sure you won't be interrupted. You can absolutely collapse aspects of ritual into shorter or longer periods of time depending on what time you have. Rest when you need to rest, and return to ritual when it feels right to you.

We often think of the ornate, arcane, and complicated when we think of ritual—and while this is certainly the case sometimes, removing barriers to ritual work means realizing time and energy is a precious thing. With this book, you won't need special, expensive, or hard-to-find objects. Only a page in your journal and a candle or two. Everything else is optional or found easily in your home.

I recommend creating a sacred writing space or altar as well (see page 44).

Showing Up for Yourself, Being Patient & Speaking Your Truth

As Mary Karr writes in her book *The Art of Memoir*, "The telling power has some magic." When we tell our truth, we are making magic. We are reclaiming our narrative, removing shame, and making it clear that our truth is worthy. The word is your numinous guide. Follow it, and you will find yourself at the precipice of change. I know because it changed my life.

Without speaking our truth, our hearts will beat in some inauthentic rhythm, dancing to a pace they don't truly understand. We owe it to ourselves and to our communities to honor our experiences, traumas, hopes, and fears. One way of doing that is to write it all down.

When you write your story—in letters or diaries or poems or in spells, you honor it, even as it changes. Our truth is an ever-changing tide, ebbing and flowing; as you move through life, your narrative will change. Ghosts come and go. Lights shine and vanish. And that's okay. Part of the magic is the discovery that comes through writing. The one constant is this: Through all of this, you will have your word and your voice. You can keep coming back to the page to honor yourself. And in doing so, there's a chance it'll help you make space for others as well. In a sense, the page is your altar of self.

By using this book, I hope you'll honor your story, even if it means returning to a ritual or to a writing prompt time and again. Magical self-exploration isn't linear. It's fluid and messy and weird. You may write something once and revisit it. You might revisit it ten times.

"Telling our stories, first to ourselves and then to one another and the world, is a revolutionary act."

— JANET MOCK

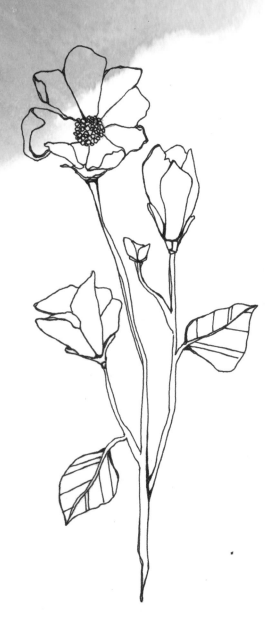

Come to the page, and to your sacred spaces and rituals, with full vulnerability and authenticity. Return to this process weekly or habitually, and it will feel more normal each time. The writing process has a way of burrowing into your skin, even if the first time feels difficult or like bleeding a stone.

I have always been comforted by the eternity of a page. It's a wildwood of opportunity and forgiveness. It's place where I can make magic. I can change a feeling of "I'm not good enough" into "I'm enough" with nothing more than self-study. I know you can too.

There is no perfect here, just tabula rasa: a blank slate from which to start again. Just write—through doubt and fear, passion and hope. Write when you don't feel like working on yourself, and write when you do. The grand ritual is that you are returning to these sacred moments.

Embracing the Magical Process

As we know, writing magic is a lifelong practice. Think of a diary—it's not the individual pages but the accumulation of your thoughts and memories that tell the whole story of you.

For this reason, this is a process-oriented book. Not every practice in this book will be aimed at Getting an Instant Result. Not every page will be a spell for this or that to get this result or that result. We have to reframe the way we think of results. Instead of lighting a candle and saying a few words written by someone else, we will light the candle, write the words ourselves (or at least many of them), and then explore the reasons why we're using these words. This empowers us and awakens us.

One of the most important lessons I've ever learned is that doing something—writing a book, casting a spell, anything—is often a process of both work and the occult.

When writing, you are tapping into the muse; this is the occult. That is the something that pours through you when you create, meditate, or write a poem. But it takes work to direct that muse. This is all a process. The result is bigger than anything immediate or obvious.

The magic is actually the change that happens within you when you direct your energy, when you show up for yourself and put in the work (even without immediate result), and when you decide to write and feel and encounter all the layers of self.

Explorations

What sort of change do you want to see in yourself? What are you afraid to write down? What are you excited to write down? Are you ready to confront and embrace the unknown? How do you envision ritual having an impact on your life? What do you want to ritualize and make sacred?

Preparing Your Mind, Body & Space for Ritual & Writing

While wordcraft can be done at any time, I think everyone should carve out time weekly for a long, intensive session of ritual and writing. Once you've found a time that works for you, create a sacred space (see page 44 on how to do this) for writing and ritual work. This space may change from time to time, and that is perfectly normal.

Mental preparation is as important—if not more so—as environmental preparation. In writing, you must strike a delicate balance between receptivity and generative energy. When we are receptive, we can conjure "the muse" or the higher self (or any spirit entities), but we must also be generative (or able to translate that energy). That is because writing is, of course, a ritual of give and take. In writing, we are translating the universe beyond and within.

We must also strike a balance between excavation and strengthening, looking to the future and remembering. Wordcraft is a sacred and cthonic practice that requires vulnerability, self-awareness, and self-care. It's not always an easy process, but it's illuminating.

To prepare for wordcraft and ritual, try some of the following practices.

BATHING

I find that bathing (through a bath or shower) is a way for me to signal to my body that I am cleansed of all energies and residues and that I am ready to write. For me, it signifies a blank page. The magic of the words, flowing through your lips or fingertips, moves freely. Take a ritual bath or simply ritualistically wash your hands before writing.

When bathing, I like to fill my bath with flower petals—often with colors associated with what I'm doing—a drop of an essential oil, some salts, or a colorful bath bomb. I also like to hang eucalyptus in my shower (I tie it around the nozzle with a rubber band or twine) to add a wonderful scent to the experience. Eucalyptus has also been used in magic to refresh, inspire, and heal.

If you can't do this for whatever reason, that is totally okay! Instead, wash your hands. You can—and should—always modify anything to your needs.

Place your hands in a bowl of water with one or two drops of lemon or lavender oil, oils known for their cleansing abilities. I like to add a crystal to the water as well. I use clear quartz or black tourmaline as symbols of cleansing. To me, both their clarity and darkness work as symbolic takers of my heaviness and callers of my light. Submerge and massage your hands within the water, grounding yourself. Take a few deep breaths and mentally prepare yourself to write honestly and clearly. Envision the day slipping out of your fingertips, absorbed and transmuted by the water.

SOMATICS

Somatics is a therapeutic practice often focused on resilience in order to deal with trauma. It integrates the body, the mind, and the environment.

Somatics asks us to be non-judgmentally aware of our bodies (this awareness is called *interoception*) rather than disconnected from them.

Practice recognizing any feelings you are inhabiting, like anxiety forming in your chest, and then source images of safety and peace to help release some tension. It can also be helpful to touch a grounding object or stretch on the floor so that you feel anchored. As you do ritual work, you'll want to keep a grounding object near you so that you can always come back to the now.

I like to use my large rose quartz. It's heavy, light pink, and soft; in short, it feels safe in my hands and sends me the message of, "you're okay."

Do some interoceptive work before ritual so that you feel embodied, alert, and aware of your emotional state. You may find that dancing and paying attention to each body part is helpful, or that breathing deeply helps you connect to yourself.

It is always helpful to enter into ritual and writing with an awareness of your body, especially if you are working with rituals that can bring up pain or remind you of traumas endured.

Designing Your Ritual Space: Accessibility & Aesthetics

We live in an era of digital curation that lets us explore the images, colors, and styles that inspire us. But we sometimes forget that we can embrace aesthetic in real life as well. We can conjure the power of aesthetic in how we dress, which fabrics we display, how we do our makeup, what music we put on, and how we design our space. Aesthetics may seem superficial, but they allow us to tap into powerful archetypes and designs that align with our intentions.

Our environments are also a huge trigger for our mental state, which is why so many immersive, meditative, ritual, or spiritual events or spaces are filled with specific kinds of decoration. A space may be adorned with greenery and flora, or with symbols of the sea and moon. It may be draped in bright colors or veiled in wood and candles. It may be minimal and airy or intimate and decorated in figures that inspire you.

Space is an invocation, so if you feel uninspired by a room, try to find another. If you feel your bedroom or writing area is leaving you feeling empty or blocked, change it. Declutter your general surroundings. Remove anything that clogs energy. Sometimes all it takes is adding something as small as some marigolds on the windowsill or a colorful throw blanket over an old couch. Sometimes a permanent or as-needed altar space makes all the difference. Sometimes candles do the trick.

Perhaps you call on the energy of the elements in your space:

Fire calls for your inner power.

Water calls for intuition, emotion, and fluidity.

Air calls for communication and planning.

Earth calls for sowing, finding foundation, and grounding.

What objects or colors invoke those qualities for you?

Whatever it is that you feel brings your space to life is what matters. Your space is an important part of your mental health and ritual work and should be treated as such. Make sure that your sacred space is accessible, comfortable, and your own. Money makes no difference. It's the intention that matters. This is the palace of you.

Humans have long adorned their sacred spaces with color, fabric, art, and intricate design.

But when it comes to witchcraft or paganism, for example, there are very little public spaces for practice, worship, or reflection— so we have to create our own, either in nature or in our bedrooms. The amazing thing about a ritualized lifestyle is that it's unique to each of us, and you are free to create an altar or space that fits your specific needs.

DESIGNING AN
INTENTIONAL ALTAR

An altar is a space (part of a bookshelf or a stand-alone area) designated for worship, magic-making, or spell work. Decorate it with items that mean something to you, as well as items used in ritual. It can be changed and redesigned to power up a particular spell or to align with a particular season, intention, or idea. Whatever you display, do so with intentionality.

Cleanse your altar and space. Use a handmade spray of water and an essential oil, like lavender. Try to use this spray for this purpose only, as it instills it with a specific meaning.

Let the literary light in. Decorate with your favorite books, hang up photos of your favorite writers, and handwrite scrolls with literary quotes.

Art and poetry. Make your own paintings, photographs, poems, drawings, and sigils and arrange them on your altar. This generative energy will fill your space with magic.

Ancestral items. Call on your heritage, ancestry, or the archetypal power of your ancestors by arranging items that invoke a country or culture. Display items handed down to you.

Decor ideas. Upside-down hanging flowers; images of figures or archetypes; tarot cards; candles in colors that speak to you; books that inspire you; figurines or paintings of creatures, deities, or archetypal figures; elemental decorations (pearls and shells, potted flowers and stones); crystals; coin dishes; bottles of wine with single flowers; comfortable pillows for meditation; sequins; food offerings; perfume bottles; fans; skulls; ancestral items.

How to Write Your Own Spells & Incantations

Before we get into rituals and writing prompts, it's important to understand the fundamentals of spell work and how you can write your own spells. A spell is a set of actions or a magical formula, especially with spoken words, intended to create a reaction.

Sometimes a spell might not work at all—but the transformation still occurs because we are doing the work behind the scenes to know ourselves and perform our magic anyway.

As a writer, I think intention and language—how it is expressed, and the rhythm and breath-work behind the speaking of the words—to be deliciously powerful. Most books offer spells to be recited, but I have always thought it useful to write your own or at least adapt spells to your own needs, cutting or keeping what most resonates with you.

I've included a few prompts here and there throughout the book to get you thinking, but I encourage you to write your own spells, short or long, whenever you can.

Every spell is a chance at autonomy, and language is autonomy.

Now, not every witch casts spells, and sometimes people who don't identify as witches do cast spells. How can that be, you may ask? Because a spell—known by many other names—is simply a way of directing energy, oftentimes punctuated by symbols and objects that carry meaning in the moment.

When I cast spells, it's often a simple affair, in terms of bells and whistles. Like a prayer or affirmation or a mantra. Like focus. Like breathing. I usually breathe until I feel tuned in, arrange a few tools in front of me (a candle, for instance) and speak a few words, pulling on a particular energy source—like flame, water, or an archetype. It can be more or even less in-depth than that. No expensive tools, no fancy clothing, and no coven necessary. It can be as simple as breath-work and stating a few words.

What is most important to me during spellcasting is that I feel focused, that I have energy to harness, and that I am directing it clearly. The right words help me achieve this state. I like to enchant my spells by beautifying my language; I often write spells as poetry and in doing so, I infuse my own creative energy with my spell work. Because creativity is magic itself—the magic of creating something out of nothing.

The more of ourselves we pour into our magic, the more power it has. Even if a spell or incantation is messy or scrawled onto a page in crayon, it is supercharged by our creativity.

In this practice, we look at the foundational ingredients or parts of a spell and focusing on the writing of an incantation for the spell.

I recommend journaling before any spell-writing: Magic—and magical journaling—helps you understand your desires and remove any latent resistance or shadow boundaries to a spell's request.

Self-interrogation (shadow work) should accompany spell-writing so you know what you truly feel.

Remember that magic is a tool for autonomy and wellness and discovery, but it can't cure illness or loneliness or oppression, for example, overnight. It can, however, help you find navigation and healing through the murk and evil in this world.

Can you journal clearly about the ways in which abundance would tangibly benefit your life?

What would that abundance even look like?

Having your needs met?

Being seen as an equal amongst your peers?

Are you living in a society that benefits from your lack of abundance?

Are you internalizing ideas about being deserving?

Although different practitioners may approach spellcraft differently, here are the general parts of the spell:

A GOAL OR INTENTION

What do you want to accomplish with this spell? This needs to be clear both during the spell work and for you. Leave no loopholes. The lifelong journey of self-exploration as a witch informs your spell work because often what we want and what we think we want are mixed up and unclear. When you come to a spell, be sure you understand repercussions.

For example

Will your spell hinder the will of another?

How might this affect you?

Will the spell bring you something that you know, deep down, is toxic or hurtful to you, but you've told yourself you need it?

Will the spell truly help you?

Is your request attainable in some way?

Magic works to bring that which can be brought. I cannot—nor can anyone else—answer these questions for you. Only time, process, and shadow work can.

AN INGREDIENTS LIST List any ingredients or tools you'd like to use, like a crystal, a candle, any objects with color, element, or other associations (like a rose petal or a bowl of water), and anything else you see fit for a spell. Remember that simplicity is as powerful as the elaborate; what matters is your intention. Objects are not arbitrary, nor are they necessary. They work as symbols and allow us to specify our intent. I find a candle helps me focus, while a crystal may symbolize something important for me.

THE TIMING Many practitioners of magic time their spell work to a moon phase, season, or day of the week. There are many books on correspondence in magic (listed in the Resources section on page 172). A moon phase guide is on page 55. While there are some exercises related to timing in the following chapters, much of this book has an emphasis on intuition. What feels right to you? Does it feel better to do your spell on a breezy Sunday morning when you have no other pressures? Or perhaps it feels better to work your magic late at night on a Friday when the energies are high and heavy?

ACTIONS Include any actions you might take (and when, if you'd like to highly structure step by step)—deep breathing, lighting incense, lighting a candle, holding a crystal, dancing, or chanting.

THE INCANTATION An incantation is a string of words or sentences used for a magical effect. This can be made of words that specify your intent. Otherwise known as a charm or a prayer, it's the words that truly conjure your intention. You might say them to yourself silently or internally (especially if you have roommates or are not in a private setting) or you may sing,

state, or scream them. You might repeat lines in order to drum up energy, or you might simply read the incantation once. You might memorize it or read it from paper. You might write conversationally or with high language. I like to focus on inflection and emphasis— which words mean the most?—as much as I like to focus on creating beautiful words and metaphors that make sense to me. Although spell-writing should be clear, if you understand your metaphors, the universe will, too. There are no hard and fast rules.

Remember to approach your spell-writing (and speaking) with musicality. As Craig Conley, quoting Thomas Moore, says in *Magic Words: A Dictionary*, "We may evoke the magic in words by their placement . . . rhyme, assonance, intonation, emphasis . . ." Your incantation can be long or short, and it can be broken into parts to allow you to focus on the various layers it might involve. Write it all down once, and then go back and edit it.

Here is a short example of a poetic incantation I use to call for healing when my autoimmune illness (chronic pain and rigidity in my bones) gets unbearable:

Water,
I ask that you bring healing to shore.
That you cleanse me of this pain.

That I am to become the expanse and the shore,
capable of both steadiness and of fluidity.
I call upon a gentleness; I call upon a softness;

I call upon your reminder that I am a thing deserving-of.
I pass along this gentle, soft thing. I pass along the sea.

Sometimes I keep it even simpler:

Water,
I ask that you heal me.
Water,
I ask that you bring me peace.

Water,
I ask to be seen.
Water,
I ask to be healed.
Water,
I promise to pass your power to others.

THE STEPS Write all the steps down one by one: When you will light the candle, when you will breathe, when you will read the incantation, and what you will do next. This is entirely up to you. Sometimes I like to dance after I state an incantation, or stretch, or simply breathe and look into the candle. Intuit this or refer to the rituals in this book for ideas.

GIVING BACK You may notice that I add lines like, "Water, I promise to pass your power to others" and "I pass along this gentleness and softness. I pass along the sea."

I believe that it is important that we use our magic not only to help ourselves but to help others. Promising to pass along goodness is, to me, a way of taking as much as I give. I may pass along the magic by sending words of love and encouragement to others, or working as an advocate for people living with chronic illness.

A note on spell work:

Spells can be part of a larger ritual, or they can be a ritual unto themselves. You can also skip any actions and just write the incantation to be read before bed or at moments during the day when you need to conjure your power.

WRITING DOWN THE MOON

Witches have always been attuned to the moon's changing phases, which may be because the moon controls the tides and we are made of water. Her bright light and surrounding darkness is a reminder that we also contain layers of self, that phases come and go, and that we, too, can change; either in our situations or in our mindsets.

To add extra intentionality and power to your magic as you move through this book, think about writing moon-timed spells or journaling during the phases of the moon. Manifestation or forgiveness spells done during a specific phase, for example, tend to be amplified. A waxing moon brings, and a waning moon releases.

Dark moon or new moon
Shadow work journaling, rewriting your narrative, establishing new writing rituals

Waxing moon
Writing manifestation spells, writing goal lists, redecorating your writing ritual space

Full moon
Setting serious written intentions and goals, journaling through high emotion, entering meditative states for writing

Waning moon
Writing goodbye letters, creating mantras of release, ridding of harmful energies, ending written projects

You Are the Chariot
Setting a Goal for Your Wordcraft Practice

The Chariot appears in the major arcana of many tarot decks. I'm particularly in love with the Chariot from The Wild Unknown deck. In the deck, the card is described as one of "strong will, achievement, triumph." To set a tone for the following rituals and practices, I believe this card allows us to focus on what we want from ourselves.

This is a card of autonomy, of moving ahead, even if we fail along the way.

In The Wild Unknown deck, the card reveals a horse, front and center, looking out into the distance, riding through the winds of change and time. This horse gallops into the future, perhaps leaving something behind. Always moving toward what is coming: creativity, joy, self-love. This card asks us to wildly gallop on. To show up for ourselves in small and big ways.

In this practice, write about what you want out of your magical writing practice. Perhaps it's to become more honest with yourself. Perhaps it's simply to start a daily writing ritual. Perhaps it's writing more magical poetry. Using the symbology of the Chariot's autonomy and triumph, I call on what you envision for yourself.

Materials

A symbol of your personal progress
A candle
Your journal
The Chariot tarot card (optional)

———————

Place upon your altar a symbol of your personal progress. I often use a photograph of myself in Mexico, when I traveled out of country for the first time in an effort to find autonomy and courage. I was frightened of flying, and even more frightened of traveling on my own for a month—with only my thoughts and memories as company. During this time, I was working through purposefully hidden PTSD symptoms due to foster care and family trauma, and this trip—funded by a year of saving—symbolized my healing.

Light a candle. Meditate on your courage and ability to make progress, whatever that looks like for you, despite setbacks. Maybe progress looks like graduation, writing a book, coming out to your peers, or simply waking up and starting the day.

Envision yourself surrounded in sparkling light, and hold the image. This may be harder for some than others, and that's okay. The self-love and self-care processes can still exist alongside our inevitable shadows. Honor them.

In your journal (on a page you can rip out), write down three ways in which you have manifested change, progressed, or galloped forward. Write them as a statement about yourself:

I am the Chariot because I _____, _____, and _____.

Rip this page out, fold it up, and carry it with you for the next three days. If you have a tarot deck with The Chariot, place it on your bedside table or your altar and meditate on it for the next three days. The three-day devotion to self is a reminder that even as the moment passes, we still have to make space to honor growth. You are still the Chariot after the ritual ends.

Creating Sigils

From the yantras of the tantric practices and apotropaic symbols used to ward off evil, to the runes of the Norse and the tattoos we get today as inked reminders of what is important to us, symbols and diagrams have long been turned to for their power. This is magic, at its most foundational level.

Consider sigils. With roots from the Latin *sigillum* (meaning "seal") and the Hebrew *segula* (meaning "a magical word"), a sigil is, simply put, a magical symbol. Sigils are generally created from the letters in a word or phrase, like "survival" or "I am abundant in creativity," along with lines, dots, and other artistic flourishes, like zodiac symbols or elemental images. Chaos magicians create sigils to represent an outcome, but sigils have also been used to summon or represent deities, like angels or demons.

There are many, many methods of creating a sigil—many arcane or traditional and many newly imagined and off the cuff. Practitioners of sigil magic often like to "forget" what they have written originally so that their subconscious minds don't prevent the magic. I do not use this method. I suggest you do some research (see Resources on page 172) and find a way that speaks to you.

To create a sigil is to create a personal, unique symbol process that, charged by your very creativity and intent, can be used for just about any purpose. This is a creative, fast, and hands-on form of magic that requires your intent—along with some paper and a pen. No one else on earth will likely make the same exact sigil as you either, as it's made up of your specific intention and energies. As you create a sigil, meditate on why you are doing so.

A common way to make a sigil is to write out a word or phrase on a piece of paper and then strike out the vowels. Use the remaining letters to create a symbol on a separate piece of paper. The resulting sigil design doesn't have to resemble the word or phrase it embodies; in fact, it can be ornamental, large, or small—and its design elements can obscure the original word or phrase. When you create a sigil, you are creating from the deep, all-powerful well of the self—to become, to manifest, to grow.

You can hang the sigil on your altar, carry it in your wallet, carve it into an object or candle, or draw it into water or earth. Many sigil users like to activate their sigil by charging it—under moonlight, or by meditating on the image itself and envisioning it being filled with power. Sigils may even activate themselves in creation, since, of course, intention carries energy. You can also light a candle as you create sigils in your sacred space.

As you move through this book, you might want to create sigils as a way to decorate and power-up your grimoire, or you might want to create one from specific lines you write in your poems or spells.

I create a sigil for each of my longer written works, including this book. It is a sacred design that hangs in my sacred writing space and reminds me of the heart of this book.

Here is my sigil for *The Magical Writing Grimoire*, made up of the letters in the title, as well as illustrated elements that I believe indicate success.

Automatic Writing
Tapping into the Liminal

*As you work through this book, you may be asked (or feel inspired)
to use automatic writing, a method of writing that asks us to enter a
different mental state in order to generate words or to channel ideas.*

*Automatic writing can help us explore the self or even channel messages
or visions from spirits, guides, ancestors, or other entities. Often
confused for free writing (in which someone simply writes whatever
comes to mind), automatic writing happens in a trance state and has
roots in spirit-conjuring sixteenth century Enochian ceremonial magic.*

*In researching for this book, I found that many poets and writers turn
to this method, often in candlelight or while burning incense. The goal
is to enter a state of trance, where they are simply the hand, and all
thoughts stream through them.*

Poet and writer Kailey Tedesco writes, in Luna Luna Magazine, *"Trance
writing, by my own personal definition, is the act of turning off the
lights in all the parts of the mind where ego, conceit, doubt, and self-
consciousness exist."*

W.B. Yeats' highly mystical work, Yeats's Poetry, Drama, and Prose
*contains poems born of the automatic writing process. According to
Yeats, this practice suspends "the conscious mind and allows the hand to
move across the paper at the behest of outside forces."*

*While Yeats felt he was connecting to something outside of himself,
automatic writing is often used in shadow work to contact your higher
self, or your shadow aspects.*

*When we use automatic writing to contact the shadow self, we write
free from censorship, shame, or judgement.*

Materials

A pen and paper
A candle

Sit somewhere comfortable, with a pen and paper. Light a candle. It is best to do this early in the morning or before bed, or whenever your mind is less noisy and more receptive.

Meditate or breathe deeply for several minutes to get your mind and body loose and ready to channel. You can repeat a mantra, follow a guided meditation, or, if you do yoga, move through poses. What act or practice feels grounding and intentional in your body? I like to stretch every limb until I'm fluid.

Breathe deeply in and out. Breathe in for five seconds, hold for five, then breathe out for five seconds. Do this for five minutes total as you stare into the flame. You can also practice envisioning a spiral of shimmering light—from the sky into your body or hands, seeing yourself falling deeper and deeper into its center. Spirals have been used throughout history, symbolizing change, deep knowledge, quintessence (or Spirit, the fifth element), intuition, nature, and cycles of life and death. In your spiral, deep in the sacred place, you can find power and grounding.

When you feel malleable and receptive, begin letting the thoughts move into and through you, as if they are circling above your head, through your skull, down your arms, and into your hands.

Do not interrupt, censor, analyze, or question the words. Write until you cannot write any longer.

Afterward, notice themes, repetitions, specific words, or feelings in your writing; from there, explore what they could mean to you.

Are they hidden feelings?

Why do you use one word over another?

Why does one theme repeat itself?

What emotion or physical sensation do the words induce?

Why might that be?

Sit in this space and contemplate, without shame or fear, your truth. You may come upon painful or hard-to-swallow realizations, but know that these, too, will pass. The only way out, as they say, is through.

EMBODYING THE ELEMENTS IN YOUR WORDCRAFT

In Latin, *elementum* translates to "first principle." Elements are at the literal core of this world and of our bodies, asking us to connect with the very foundation of all things. Throughout this book, you'll be writing with elemental magic.

Water asks us to seek depth, fluidity, intuition, emotionality, and shadowy layers of self.

Write a poem that reflects your deepest, most hidden fear; by writing it you confront it.

Earth asks us to ground ourselves, find stability, plant seeds, and seek patience and peace in process.

Write a goal on a small piece of paper and plant it in soil with a seedling. Grow the flower on your windowsill and give life to your dreams.

Wind asks us to transcend higher, to think freely, to seek open spaces and new ideas, and to release.

Write a letter to your future self, asking yourself to hear you and to understand you. How do they respond? Speak it into the air.

Fire asks us to tap into our pure power, bravery, sensuality, and engine-like drive.

Write a list of things you want to call forth or banish, and set it on fire in a fire-proof bowl near a sink.

As you journal through this book, do you need to call on fire? Perhaps you need air's expansiveness? Can water help you fill your depths? Tap into the elements as you write; they serve as guides and points of inspiration.

In water, we intuit.

In air, we expand.

In earth, we grow.

In fire, we create.

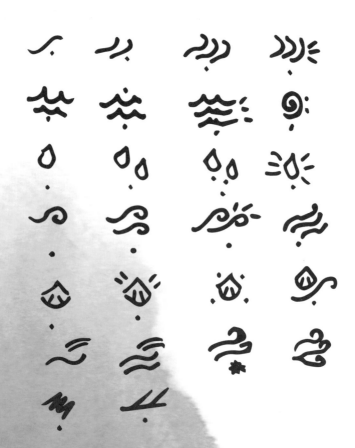

THE MAGICAL WRITING GRIMOIRE

Creating Your Own Magical Alphabet

Many practitioners of magic have, over time, created their own alphabets. These alphabets were used to record and obscure magical content, but some alphabets were simply used as a form of communication. An alphabet is usually specific to the cultures in which they were created.

Creating your own alphabet forces you to slow down and focus intently on both creating a set of letters and translating writings into your own unique language. This amplifies the energy put into writing (and then decoding) a spell in your grimoire or a wish statement to be placed on an altar, for example. The more focus, the better.

Decide what kind of design you'd like to use. Some alphabets contain lines, others dots, some star-like characters. As a witch that works with water, I have created one based on ocean waves. You can see mine opposite.

Once you've decided on the look of your alphabet, you may create symbols or images that represent ideas, concepts, or desires. Or, you can associate each image with a letter in the alphabet you speak. Create a clear and easy-to-understand key to work from. You can then use your alphabet to write spells, incantations, dreams, or written works that hang in your altar space. (This is especially helpful if you have, *ahem*, nosy roommates who like to read things they're not supposed to read.)

Should you want to use alphabets from other cultures, be aware of using ones that are part of a closed culture—meaning, practices performed by a specific community or tribe of which you are not a part. Not everything is available to us just because we *want* to use it. For inspiration, though, it's worth investigating some of the alphabets used throughout history, like the Malachim or Enochian alphabets. Also beautiful are the Mayan glyphs, cuneiform symbols, and the Celtic tree alphabet.

Graphology: Understanding Your Handwriting

Before you begin writing spells, working through journaling prompts, and filling out your grimoire, consider looking at your handwriting through the lens of graphology, which is the study of handwriting.

According to the British Institute of Graphologists, "Handwriting is the pattern of our psychology expressed in symbols on the page and these symbols are as unique as our own DNA." Every slant, angle, and space means something.

In fact, humans have long turned to handwriting as a way of decoding an individual's personality. In 500 BCE, Confucius stated, "Beware of a man whose writing sways like a reed in the wind." Later, in seventeenth century Italy, graphology became a recognized study of human nature and identity.

For example, if we write in smaller letters, are we hiding something—either from ourselves or from others? If we use larger letters, are we trying to get something out of ourselves? If we slant our words up and toward the right, are we sending something out into the cosmos? Do you cram your words in, side by side? Perhaps you are too rigid? Open spaces between words denote flexibility, openness, creativity. As you write, assess your handwriting and the reason you write the way you do. If you write in your grimoire, or write mantras or incantations that you display on your altar, for example, how does your handwriting contain or express your intention?

See Resources on page 172 for more on decoding graphology.

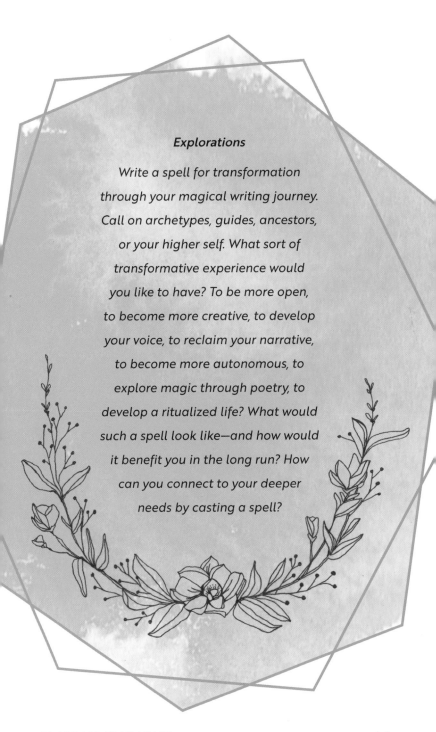

Explorations

Write a spell for transformation
through your magical writing journey.
Call on archetypes, guides, ancestors,
or your higher self. What sort of
transformative experience would
you like to have? To be more open,
to become more creative, to develop
your voice, to reclaim your narrative,
to become more autonomous, to
explore magic through poetry, to
develop a ritualized life? What would
such a spell look like—and how would
it benefit you in the long run? How
can you connect to your deeper
needs by casting a spell?

CHAPTER 3
HEALING MAGIC

Rituals and Writing
Prompts for Shadow Work,
Trauma Recovery, and
Transformation

You stand on a jetty, long and thin, stretching far out into a deep and wild sea. On either side of the jetty, water for miles. Behind you is the shore. The water to the right is dark, wild, onyx glass. But the water to the left is blue and bright, foamy and translucent. As you stare out into the waters, the black overtakes the blue. Then the blue pushes the black back, back, away. There is no good, no bad, no dark water that can't heal, and no blue water that can't ruin. And yet. Words form upon the water's surface on either side. What are they? What are they telling you? Do you feel that darkness is the enemy? Is there something in the water that you are running from? Is trust only gained in the things we know to be real and good and true—or can you dive into the mystery? What messages do you receive here on this precipice? What does it feel like to stand at the crossroad of the sea and the self?

" I write to create myself. "

— OCTAVIA E. BUTLER

One of the most beautiful things about adopting a magical practice is that we can create a safe space according to our own needs in which we can explore our wounds. We can ritualize our healing process, making it sacred. When we write, we name our ghosts and demons.

The ancient Egyptians believed that names wield power—and to know a person's name is a powerful thing. When we know the names of our many selves— pain, jealousy, fear—it gives us power over them. Rather than keeping them in dark, where they fester from within like a poison, we let the light illuminate them. When you can truly *see* what has been wounding you, it loses some of its ability to haunt you in the dark. You can then take action against it.

In this chapter, you will name your darkness and bring light into the spaces where only shadow has lived.

On Practicing Healing Magic—Without Even Knowing It

Here's a bit about my story, and how I began integrating writing and magic into my healing process—before I even realized that was what I was doing. I grew up in New Jersey, in a small town that had roots back to the Revolutionary War.

When I was eleven or twelve—the memory is hazy—after my parents had separated due to addiction issues, my brother, mother, and I moved into my grandmother's one-bedroom apartment at a senior citizen complex. Later, we'd end up in homeless shelters and, after that, foster care.

For many years, I either shared a bed with my grandmother or my brother. At one point, we lived in a single-window bedroom at the YMCA; summers meant going to rehab and counseling with my mother. Nights meant Alcoholics Anonymous meetings in lofty, melancholy churches. Without knowing it, I developed a sort of psychological and physical claustrophobia, constantly made to live with strangers or crowded in a small room with my family. It felt increasingly hard to find my own way when I was always managing the trauma. I internalized this, and tucked myself away from others in many ways.

I wouldn't realize it until more than a decade later, but the trauma of addiction, family destruction, and poverty had a lasting effect on me. The lack of personal space, the fever dream of constant trauma, of being uprooted over and over and over again, and the loneliness of different schools and houses chipped away at my sense of autonomy. I was defined by a constant sense of lack or longing, my childhood stolen from me. And even though I don't blame my parents for their disease, I admit that I long for different memories.

Within this pain, I had a space of my own: a small diary with a lock. I wrote every single day, and

> *" The wound is the place*
> *where the light enters you. "*

— R U M I

about everything. I wrote every secret, every confession, every burst of rage.

We lived mostly in urban environments, but over the years I'd turn to a park, or the woods behind our complex, or a shallow river passing through town, and I'd let nature guide me. This finding nature didn't feel like magic. It was subconscious. Intuitive.

The elements provided an acute sense of meaning that I somehow understood; through whatever pain I was feeling, the elements comforted me. Nature was generous and forgiving, soft and separate from the harsh reality of people and poverty. And like the poets before me, nature sung through me, giving me a creative muse that allowed me to separate from the pain and create something beautiful.

I'd write poems about water or short stories about faeries and butterflies. These natural things allowed me to talk about myself and my problems metaphorically. They gave me a way to confront the depths.

I remember writing once, "I am a river leading to the sea." I now know what it meant: I was conjuring something bigger, something more beautiful.

Sitting in the park, I'd write my wishes and my hopes for my mother and father. I'd sketch pictures of dream homes. I wrote of places I wanted to visit. Without knowing it, I was making word magic—pulling my life to me. And I was healing myself, slowly.

When I let my fingers brush against the flowers and the water and the rocks like dancing beasts at the beach, I was learning another language. It was the language of magic and autonomy and healing, but I wouldn't practice speaking it—or making magic—for many, many years. Instead, that magic, of nature and beauty, burrowed into my heart and bloomed when I was ready.

When did magic begin to call your name? Why?

How do the elements speak to you? What heals you?

What secrets or hidden feelings or fears are emerging?

If you pulled back the curtain of the self, what would you find?

What would it look like to heal?

What would an environment or space look like that could heal you?

How can you create that space?

What words would you write to the wound within you?

Write them, and speak them out loud.

Shadow Work, Trauma Recovery & Allowing Yourself Magic and Healing

Often, when we work on healing our shadow selves, a huge part of our pain comes from the external: unfair systems and institutions, parents who abandoned us, assault, systemic poverty, or social oppression. When we try to heal, we cannot blame ourselves for not forgiving or moving on. These wounds are deep and impactful and they affect us individually, generationally, and in our communities.

If there is a huge rift between the traumas you've endured and the power you have over them, you may feel compelled to heal them. This process is not perfect nor linear, nor is it cinematic or even pleasant. It can be gradual and quiet.

Is there something you are trying to heal from that has a deeper root? Honor that in your rituals and in your writing by acknowledging it and making a space for it outside of your body. As I wrote in *Light Magic for Dark Times*, the only way to stop the suffering is to feel the pain.

When the tide is high, it's harder to swim to shore, but that doesn't mean you'll never reach a semblance of safety, even within a broken system. In ritual and in writing, we don't eliminate evil or hardship. But we do find our safe spaces, our voices, and the ways in which we sustain our bodies and minds even when darkness surrounds us.

From this moment forward, permit yourself to heal. To try these exercises. To understand darkness. To embrace your own light.

The Goodbye Letter
A Waning Moon Practice

In the practice of sympathetic magic, one uses "imitation" or likeness as a source of power. If you burn an object, you are destroying its hold on you. If you grow a flower in soil that has been charged with the energy of self-growth, you grow as it grows. And if you practice waning moon magic, you release that which doesn't serve you, as the moon slowly disappears from the sky.

The moon is waning between the full moon and the new moon. As it grows darker and darker, ending its luminous cycle, write a goodbye letter.

The moon's ultimate enchantment is its constant reminder that things change: Tides change, times change, and the light that we let in or give off changes day to day and week to week. Transformation happens naturally and constantly, and the moon allows us to lean into that.

Practice this monthly, right around the time when the moon darkens— just before the new moon, when energies of newness and opportunity take hold, leaving space for you to flourish and welcome new ideas. This practice doesn't require a ritual, although I often like to take a long, hot bath, cleaning myself of the residue of the past few weeks (or years) before writing.

Use this practice as a way to part with the past month's stressors and heartaches, or whenever you feel your ghosts beckoning at the door or getting rowdy and rancorous in the cracks of your psyche.

Materials

Your journal
Fireproof bowl
Matches or a lighter

———————————

When you sit to write your goodbye letter, address it to whatever it is that you'd like to part with—shame, depression, inability to forgive, nonstop stress, self-hatred—whatever it may be.

Begin by writing, "Dear [insert emotion or idea]," and go from there. The important thing is that you write the letter without judgement or censorship; you might not be able to say the darkness out loud or to other people, but you can say it to paper.

Are there things you feel need to be reframed or honored—even if they don't feel good?

Can you grant yourself forgiveness?

Can you say goodbye to your imposter syndrome by not only saying it's unnecessary but understanding the root of why you feel it?

End the letter with a goodbye—a parting from whatever it is you need to move on from:

I say goodbye to shame. I put shame to bed. I am no longer shameful. I honor the time in my life in which I let shame lead me, but it no longer has a place in my life.

Burn the letter in a fireproof bowl near the sink, watching the fire carry away the goodbye. Honor yourself, and the time you spent to detangle yourself from your shadows, by playing some music, dancing, eating, or breathing through the appreciation of your humanity.

Climbing into the Abyss
A Ritual for Questioning Your Most Limiting Beliefs

In this practice, we look toward something called proprioceptive writing *for inspiration.*

When we engage proprioceptive writing, we are listening to our minds and conveying exactly what we feel onto paper. The in-between thoughts are conveyed as well: What am I feeling? Why do I feel silly writing this? I am feeling fear around writing this topic, and here's why . . .

In this practice, we are going to deconstruct beliefs that we hold to be true about ourselves or others—beliefs that hold us back, keep us in shadow, keep us lonely, inflexible, or self-harming. These beliefs might be that we are inherently undeserving, that all people are out to hurt us, or that we aren't capable. What are your limiting beliefs?

Beliefs I've worked through include my belief that I lack some magical essential quality—HINT: It doesn't exist!—that helps me to fit in with or be loved by others. Through proprioceptive writing, I've followed that belief down a rabbit hole on the page:

I feel like I don't fit in with others. I feel like they see me as weird. They see me as weird because I'm wearing the face of trauma; I seem too sad or too hard or not sweet enough or not presentable enough.

But why do I have to seem untarnished to be liked? Who goes through life untarnished? Why would trauma make them not like me? Because trauma is embarrassing. Because I want to be perfect. Why would pain be embarrassing? Why is trauma bad? Trauma has made me compassionate. Compassion is likable. No one is perfect. Why would they hold me to these standards? Why am I holding myself to them? Do I feel bad for letting my trauma make me self-conscious?

And so forth. If you can question yourself, answer yourself, and then ask further questions along the way, you can examine your psyche in a way that allows you to see yourself from all angles.

The goal is that you approach even your limitations from the point of compassion and rugged honesty. Once you let go of the assumptions, mythologies, and ideas of reality that you have built, you can free yourself to adjust your mindset.

Materials

A single candle
A moonstone
Your journal

———————————

Light a single candle, and simply sit comfortably holding your moonstone. The moonstone, with its associations to the moon itself, is considered protective, luminous, and healing; symbolic of deep waters and depths of self.

Let yourself breathe deeply, feeling the moonstone between your fingers. Let its energy and symbolic power inspire you to let go, to drift deeper and deeper into the palace of you.

In proprioceptive writing, writers usually complete their writing by candlelight, free of distraction, for twenty-five minutes. Write through this time, following your thoughts and engaging them as they crop up. Don't silence or censor them.

At the end of your writing experience, meditate on the thoughts you've had and what you've learned. Be sure to show yourself gratitude for your work.

Writing Your Liminality
An Amulet-Charging Ritual for Honoring Your Many Layers

We all contain multiple layers. We all inhabit joy and hope and beauty, just as we play host to jealousy, fear, and lurking secrets. What are the names of our in-between selves? Do they have the space to flourish?

Why can't we be the sinner and saint at once? Which archetypes can we fold into one glorious new being?

Look at Hecate, polymorphous night goddess, as she marches through the crossroads and dark realms lit with a torch. In her hand, the sacred key. She asks us to walk into the abyss, to wander through the dark, into the light, and back again. And in her moonlit glow, we can illuminate and honor every part of ourselves—the lost parts, the shadow parts, the loud parts, the tender parts. You are allowed to be all of them at once.

Call on Hecate's guidance to illuminate all of it—and all the shadowy bits in between—and write it down.

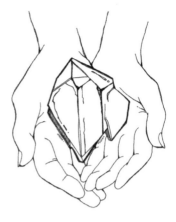

Materials

A single black candle
A crystal (such as black tourmaline,
    black onyx, or smoky quartz)

Light a single black candle to
illuminate your many selves. Stand
before it for several moments, calling
on your shadow and your light
without censor, without shame,
without justification, and without
judgement.

Deeply breathe—inhale for five
seconds, exhale for five seconds—
several times, until you feel connected
to the moment.

Call out your many selves: Honor
your multiple layers. Think of all
the selves you are and bless each
of them by sending them love and
compassion. Let your body lead you in
this worship.

Write your selves into your journal in
a list, or in a poem. As you write them,
sit with them. Let them stir within
you, heard and seen. Let them haunt
and inhabit you.

Hold your stone (the crystals
mentioned above are all associated
with Hecate, stones that protect and
honor liminality and can retain our
darkness and power) and charge it
with who you are.

This object is now an amulet that
represents your ability to hold space
for your multitudes, to let them guide
you through change and healing.

Here is a piece from my journal:

In my body the playful, the sinful, the nude, the prude, the hungry, the fillable, the crash-the-party, the stay at home, the sick, the swimmer, the slut, the lover, the Catholic, the witch, the leader, the introvert, the quick-tongued, the quiet one, the hopeful, the hopeless, the traumatized, the reborn, the healer, the wounded, the weirdo, the girl who fits in, the girl who hates, the girl who loves, the not girl, the girl, the not woman, the woman, the nothing and the everything, the crossroads, the way home, the duality, the liminal, the transcendence.

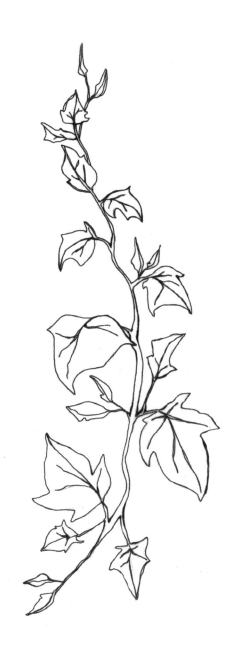

Shedding Old Skin
Writing a Eulogy for the Past

In Women Who Run with the Wolves, *a must-read book by Dr. Clarissa Pinkola Estés, poet, writer, and cantadora, she describes the idea of "descansos." These are little white crosses often found by the side of the road in Mexico, the Southern American states, Greece, Italy, and various other countries. They mark where someone's life ended. Often they are decorated by those who remember the deceased.*

Estés explores descansos in her work by writing out the journey of her life, from beginning to present, on a large piece of paper. Over the days of death, loss, transformation, pain, or suffering she lays a cross (or an x or a heart, whatever you'd like). These are places that need to be mourned, forgiven, released.

As she brilliantly writes in her book, "Descansos is a conscious practice that takes pity on and gives honor to the orphaned dead of your psyche."

Perform this practice in a ritual environment, adorned with flower petals, lighting a single candle for each bend in the road, helping the dead little memories and stagnant hopes and jagged endings find their way out of limbo and into a place of rest. This practice allows you to celebrate your life and your trajectory, despite your pain.

" *Tears are words that need to be written.*"

—— PAULO COELHO

Materials

An altar space
A bag of small votive candles
Flower petals of any variety,
    in colors that speak to you
Several small pieces of paper
    (however many you need)

Arrange an altar space to use for this practice only. I recommend you do this on a weekend or during a time you won't be interrupted. You will be creating a funeral for that which has never been properly buried or mourned, use space that feels safe and clear from interruption. Sacred.

In silence, sketch out the journey of your life. Childhood. Adolescence. Memories of loss. Pain. Grief. Being made to feel invisible. Being abandoned. Having to persevere without assistance, support, a friend. Having to wear the mask of survival when you've been beaten down. Times in which poverty or illness or systemic oppression cut your path short. Eras in which you were alone. Homes in which you felt scared. The map-making of your life is a changing process.

I like to fill in my chart with my beautiful moments later on, after I've properly mourned for what I've lost and suffered.

Next, write each of your eras, memories, homes, or moments onto a piece of a paper and cross them out. This should be symbolic, sacred. Breathe through it. Light a single candle for each, and arrange flower petals (or any other symbolic or aesthetic items, like crystals) around the paper and the candle. You may choose other religious or spiritual relics as well. Intuit this. Beautify the graves of the selves. Take time for each and every one that you write.

Don't play into the gloom if that's not your way. Instead you can play the music you used to love, talk to your old self, laugh about their mistakes. There is room for it all. The mourning process plays out differently for each of us.

I have looked upon my map of self and said, at each point, "You are loved and laid to rest." Perhaps there is another way for you to say goodbye—in your own language out loud, in a poem, or in a unique statement you write for yourself. If you wrote your own letting go spell, what would it look like?

Creating a Confessional Ritual
Giving Your Shadows a Name

The ancient Egyptians believed in the power of names. In this ritual, you name your shadows and call them out by the name you give them. The shadow contains everything from ego and phobia to trauma and stagnation. It's the dark mansion of what we do to ourselves and what's been done to us. The shadow is not a bad thing. It's a dark thing. There's a difference.

When it comes to confessing our shadows, doing so in a ritualized setting makes our confession sacred. The religious concept of a confessional, as we know it today, is centuries old. Some form of confession occurs throughout many religions, though not all. For some, the idea of confession is freeing; for others, it's rooted in ideas of shame and judgement. Confession may differ for each of us, but I think of it as (sometimes brutal) honesty with the self.

When we validate and honor our darkness, we can begin to heal it.

Maybe you want to confess being an unavailable friend or thinking bad thoughts about someone you barely know. These are the things that make us human. The things that come from trauma or pain or just straight-up feral cattiness.

In choosing to confess the stagnant, poisonous shit we hold inside of us, we call to a lineage of witches and accused witches who were forced to make true or untrue confessions, often to a fatal end. We have the opportunity to reclaim the confession.

Rather than confessing to a god because we are sinful and bad and requiring forgiveness, we are confessing our demons and shadows to ourselves. That said, if you'd like to call on a god, goddess, ancestor, angel, or deity of any kind in your practice, please do!

This is an embracing of the shadow, and an exercise that opens up your ability to be more empathic and forgiving toward yourself and others.

Explorations

Are there shadow aspects that can transmorph or be used for good? Are there shadow aspects you must for-give? Are there shadow aspects that are sticking around, no matter how hard you work? Why are they stuck? What can you do to gently let them go? What accountability can you take? What can you do to be softer to yourself? In your journal, make a note on how to do the above. Simply by naming your shadows and medi-tating on them, you have taken that dark energy and transformed it into potential. This energy becomes one of change.

Materials

A shower, bath, or bowl of cleansing
  water
A single white candle used only for
  this confession
A large jar or box with a lid (decorative
  or otherwise)
Small strips of paper
Black yarn

Late at night, when the worries of the day are over and you can sit alone and in silence, take a purifying bath or shower (or wash your hands), and enter your sacred space. Turn off the lights and light a single white candle, allowing it to flicker and dance.

Gaze into the flame, speaking your confession out loud. You can call on or confess to a deity here or simply confess to yourself. You might speak something like:

I confess Judgement, the beast that hungers in the dark. I confess its name, my name. I confess it as a part of me, a part that I control.

*In my naming you,
you cannot have me.*

Open your jar or box (and make sure you only use it for confessions). I have a floral, lidded pink glass jar I bought in Spain, but you may use whatever is right for you. Write the confession on a slip of paper, roll it into a scroll, tie the black yarn around the paper and slip it into your confession jar or box. Black, contrary to what some might say, is very luminous; it wards off negativity and protects us. It holds us in its strength.

The use of black yarn draws a boundary between you and the deeper pain that your confession may cause you. It allows you to control your shadows so that they don't dim your entire life. The use of yarn gives your confession a physicality that can help pull your body's energy into your spell work.

This container provides a space for your shadows and demons, honoring them as a part of you. In a society that values keeping secrets, even from ourselves, and burying our quirks, flaws, and weaknesses so that we present as neat and tidy, healing takes place when you show up to your truth, in a sacred setting, where you are in control.

Astrological Shadow Work: Healing Writing Prompts for Every Sign

Astrology helps us look at the many luminous (and sometimes limiting) narratives of humanity. Hanging above us in the stars in an illustrated fabric of what it means to be human: To want, to hurt, to self-destruct, to transform, to find justice, to intuit, to survive. You don't need to "believe" in astrology. Like tarot, these narratives offer a system within which to reflect. I even co-host a podcast called *Astrolushes*, in which I discuss astrology. By the way, I'm a Scorpio, if you couldn't tell.

And because each and every sign offers lessons on our potential and on our limitations, you can use these prompts in several ways: You can work with the prompts for your sun, moon, or rising signs. The moon also enters a different sign every two days or so, meaning you can always use the moon's move through the zodiac to reflect on each sun sign.

If you don't have any Scorpio in your chart, for example, you can still use its prompt; just wait for the days when the moon enters Scorpio. (Check the Resources section on page 172 for an app to help you with this).

ARIES What, in your triumphant, hard blaze, are you hiding from? Is there a softness you can grant yourself? What would it look like if you could undress in the light of flexibility? Does it pay to hold tight and remain stoic, or are you limiting yourself?

TAURUS What happens when ugliness seeps in? What will you do to honor it without losing yourself? Can you handle the lack? What happens when there's nothing around to beautify the void? What can you bring out of yourself, organically?

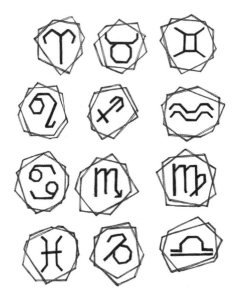

GEMINI When you silence or suppress one part of yourself, how does it feel? How can you worship at the feet of your multitudes? How can you become a chameleon without losing yourself? What does your foundation look like?

CANCER When you are unsafe, can you find an anchor? If the sea keeps rocking, how can you find your strength without capsizing? How can you learn to let nostalgia bloom without its vines suffocating you? What does safety feel like inside your body?

LEO Sometimes, you are so busy roaring you don't hear the small sounds of morning and night. Meditate on this. What's in front of you? What happens when the radiance machine stops working? Can there be power in the darkness? How can you be proud of yourself when your crown falls off?

VIRGO In the chaos, there is a song. What does it sound like? Outside the lines, you find yourself. When you are shapeless, what are you free to become? Can you find worth in the wildness, or hold space for the imperfect self? What happens when you dismantle the cliché?

LIBRA What can you learn about yourself when you feel imbalanced? Is there authenticity to be found when you're not busy balancing and performing, seeking and connecting? What is found beneath the robe—and then beneath even that? Who are you when everyone goes home?

SCORPIO You feel the hum of power in the dark, but are you the architect of your own misery? Do you stay guarded in the shadows because it's safer than letting the light in? Part the curtains. What can grow when you learn to differentiate the well from the water? What happens when you stop being jealous of the sky?

SAGITTARIUS How can you learn what it feels like to stay—with others, with yourself—when you always want to keep moving? Are you running? What happens when the ideas and the wanderlust leave you empty? What happens when you stop wearing the mask? Who are you when you take the wings off and stand still?

CAPRICORN Imagine the wild, wide desert. You are lost. You are thirsty. You are rescued. What happens when you learn to drink from someone else's palm? Can you find peace in needing someone or something other than yourself? Can you lean into the softness, the slowness? Who are you when you aren't in control?

AQUARIUS Can you operate deep underground? Can you burrow into the murky waters of fear and love and want? What happens when you get naked and sit in the garden of your dark? When you don't have a bird's-eye view, when you *comeinrealcloselikethis* can you feel the granules? What do they feel like?

PISCES What does it look like when you step out of the dream world? Can you remain here, and now, when fantasy and reality fail to merge? Can you intuit yourself? Are you able to hold space for your hopes—without crumbling under their impossible beauty? When you look your self-destruction in the face, what do you say to it?

" I am flesh, bones
I am skin, soul
I am human
Nothing more than human
I am sweat, flaws
I am veins, scars
I am human
Nothing more than human "

———————— SEVDALIZA

"Just as a snake sheds its skin, we must shed our past over and over again."

— BUDDHA

Body Poetics

A Ritual & Chant for Self-Healing After Trauma

When we experience trauma—whether it is rooted in chronic illness, verbal abuse, assault, gender violence, or something else—it lives within us. It doesn't matter if it's recent or if it happened "years ago"; what matters is the indelible and often invisible scars it leaves within us, be they raw and painful or repressed. What matters is how they quietly unravel in us. What they take from us.

When our bodies and minds learn the language of trauma, we change on a deep level. A report in Psychology Today *found that early trauma, especially, rewires the brain, leaving lasting cognitive and emotional effects. We are only human. We are beings that get hurt again and again. It is natural, but that doesn't mean we have to accept our pain as something we cannot control.*

In this practice, you will confront the trauma in a safe space— and in a repetitious manner. Choose a day that you can devote each week to your ritual; it is important that self-healing be ritualized and repetitive so that you can both honor your strength while rewiring those pathways. Showing up for yourself each week is incredibly empowering.

You may never be able to heal completely—and this is something most people don't admit to themselves—but you will be able to grow flowers from all that fucked up soil. Think of the resilience of the earth. Think of the little flower that unfurls from the cement. That's you. It's messy and it's nonlinear, but its potential can never, ever be taken from you.

Materials

Your journal

A bath

Candles to place around your body in a circle

A grounding item, like a flower

First, write a few words to yourself. Use these words as a repetitive chant, a string of words that you can memorize and repeat, working yourself into a trance state as you say them out loud. Focus on each and every word, taking them into your body. Remember to focus on words that make you feel good. Colors, adjectives, and metaphors should be chosen with care. Intuit which words feel right. Do you prefer an angrier chant? Do you prefer one of beauty and softness? There is no wrong way to do it.

After you've written your chant, take comfort in a self-loving bath full of bath salts, flower petals, and anything else you'd like. Imagine as the water drains that your pain is being pulled with it.

Next, create your sacred space. Surround yourself with single candles, which should illuminate you from all angles, bringing the trauma out into the light. Have a grounding object with you—something of the earth that reminds you to be present, reminds you that you are safe and no longer in the past; that you are rooted.

When you are ready, deeply breathe and read from your hand-written chant. Repeat it until you memorize it and feel comfortable sinking into the words. Play with whispering it, singing it, or chanting it rhythmically.

Repeat it as you envision your body filled with shimmering, healing light, cleansing out the dark, dim, heavy, chaotic, shameful, sad spots, replacing them with love and peace.

Your body will feel full and luminous when you are finished; just be sure to come back to this ritual as often as you need. You can write a different chant each time. Save your chants in your grimoire or hang them on your altar.

Here is my chant:

My heart is a house of open windows; my body is a garden. I am ivy growing in perpetuity. I am forever of the breeze. My heart is a house of safety, my body a garden.

A Letter to Your Younger Self

For this ritual and writing prompt, you will examine the inherent power of letter writing—as a tool for reconciliation, healing, closure, acceptance, and honor. Sometimes this healing comes from forgiveness or love—and sometimes, these words come from rage, jealousy, and fear.

To prep, think on your childhood, your teen years, and who you are now. What was lost? What had to go? What remains? Who we are now has changed so much from who we were. At the same time, there are things that have a lasting impact, good and bad. Ghosts linger. Sometimes that ghost is you.

Our traumas, our growth, our pain, our losses, our loves, our whimsies, our accomplishments— these are the things we'll be writing to in this practice. Writing these letters can help us honor and heal our old selves, and by doing this, we can heal who we are today.

Light a candle. Look into the flame and take note of what thoughts arise when you think upon your younger self. As you look at the flame, conjure the person you were. Quietly welcome them into the room. What are they wearing? What are they feeling?

Choose a memory or an era in your life and write a letter to yourself. What is the goal? Is it to remind your younger self of the love they have but have never felt? Is it to congratulate them on their resilience? Is it to say that their weakness and struggles were beautiful? Perhaps you will pull a tarot card to find illumination or specificity in this process. Perhaps you will think on how your birth chart influenced the person you were. Life goes by so quickly. We are so busy existing in the middle of it that we rarely look back and study what happened:

What went right?

What went wrong?

What led to who you are now?

What would you tell your younger self?

How did they feel in their bodies—and how has this changed?

What do you want them to let go of?

Here is my letter, as an example:

Lisa Marie, at fifteen you were so lost and so sad. You moved from homeless shelter to homeless shelter, from one foster home to another—always looking for an anchor. Within your heart lived a thousand hopes and goals but they felt too hard to attain in the chaos. You were excited to write, to study, to live—and yet you always felt held back by the need to survive trauma. In you, a darkness grew. That darkness was your fuel, but it also hurt you. You had no control over it, no way to lean into it for good. You had self-esteem issues, you often felt alone. Unworthy. Angry. But you had such steadfast determination and such a good heart. You were many things, once you let the anger and fear unfurl: Soft. Empathic. Adaptable. Liminal. Able to balance the darkness and the luminous. You found poetry and magic and ritual, and you created this book that you are writing right now. Don't believe that the sadness stays forever. It doesn't.

What does your letter say?

Restorative Grief: Letters to the Dead

In *The Art of Death: Writing the Final Story*, Edwidge Danticat writes with profound openness about her mother's death. The book explores writings about death in some effort to explain how to write it, diving right into the heart of the matter. Danticat mentions Mary Gordon's memoir, *Circling My Mother*, in which Gordon states that writing was the only way she could mourn her mother: Gordon described her writing about her mother as an *active grief*.

And this rings true. Some grief is inert. Some grief is an engine. Sometimes actively participating in grief is one small way that we can learn to escape its riptide. In a way, when we mourn and when we write, we are weaving an indelible memory. We do something with the grief. We actively move through it.

Three years ago, I lost two family members who were very close to me. The grief was tidal, and I was at sea. Nights were underscored by anxiety around what I could have or should have done, obsession on mortality and meaning, and nostalgia like a drunken swirl. My days were hazy, weary, long. At work, I was distracted. At home, I was restless. I was caught between trying to live and trying to let go.

So I started writing letters to the dead. You may want to write them and keep them, or write them and then burn or bury them, pulling the wound out of your body and putting it onto paper.

In your practice, look to Seshat, an Egyptian funerary goddess (also, of course, a goddess of writing and books). Seshat, described in texts as being pregnant with the deceased, was responsible for keeping the memory of the dead alive by writing down accounts of their life.

We can tap into the ancient, beautiful archetype of Seshat, letting her dedication to the dead inspire the eulogies we write.

The very act of embracing your feelings around death, summoning the memories of your dead, and inviting them into your space through the page is powerful; it is a conjuring on many levels. And it is an essential way of embracing the death positive philosophy, which encourages people to speak openly about death, dying, and corpses. While no philosophy can remove the eternal sting of grief, this philosophy helps to lessen the shame, fear, confusion, and stigma attached to death and grief.

Choose who to write to, and what you want to say. Do you have a photograph of them? If so, place it before you. Create an altar dedicated to them, if that feels right to you. It might include things they owned, or anything that represents them. Light a black candle (They are powerful healing tools) and look into the flame. Think of this flame as illuminating a way for the dead to come home, to you, to your room, to your side.

Sit with them for a while.

What was it about them that stands out to you?

What was it you never said?

What do you wish you knew about them?

What was it you wish you did with them?

What are their quirks?

What fabric did they love?

What perfume?

How did they look when they entered the room?

What did they sing to themselves?

What's your loveliest memory of them?

If they did anything to inspire you, what was it?

What did they love?

What mark did they leave when they left this earth?

Some grief is even more complex. Perhaps the person who passed away was someone who hurt you but whom you still mourn. If so, acknowledge this. What did they do to hurt you? What have they done that has never been resolved? How has it hurt you? Can you forgive them? Can you work on forgiveness? There is no shame in not reaching forgiveness; this is a personal act.

Open the letter, "Dear [NAME]," and then continue naturally. You can remain in the positive, or tell them everything you miss about them. You may want to tell them the hard truth; you may want to let the rage out of its tiny, silenced box. Or maybe you want to tell them it's okay to go. The letter can be structured or wild. This is up to you.

The important thing is that you're honest and that you say everything you want to say. Maybe you make it a point to write to them with each new moon, or on their birthday.

On staying afloat in the ocean of grief: If you are afraid of the darkness and grief involved here, keep your environment comfortable and comforting. Have objects of happiness and safety around you. Make sure you have a support system on speed dial. Take care of yourself afterward. Because part of diving into the abyss is knowing your way out.

Explorations

Write a spell that calls for closure. Perhaps your spell invokes the elements or archetypes, or perhaps it's a spell-poem that is simply a goodbye. When we write our own spells for healing, we begin an important process—that which gives us control over the situation and the narrative, and that which enables us to embody who we want to become after trauma. What would your closure spell look like? Will it explore forgiveness? Binding? Saying goodbye? Will it honor your pain?

CHAPTER 4
MANIFESTATION MAGIC

Rituals and Writing
Prompts for Setting
Intentions and Harnessing
Your Power

Before you, a garden. Everywhere you look there are vines and thick curtains of green. Hydrangeas and honeysuckle, birdsong and ancient fountains trickling. Pathways of velvet petals and the glittering remnants of rain that fell not an hour ago. You can still sense it hovering in the sweet air. What color is the sky here? How many types of flowers can you find? As you move, you get deeper and deeper into the lush, velvety green. Finally, without direction or aid, you find a bonfire, lit and wild, dancing, orange. It is contained but unattended. It is all yours. It is for you. Stare into the flames and let its heat sing to you. If you look deep enough, you will see words emerge. What do they say? What is the message? What can you create if you look into the flame? What image can you conjure in its energy? How far can you let yourself wander into the garden of possibility? What can you do to nourish the garden? Can you call for the rain, the sun, and the stars?

Manifestation:
Conjuring & Creating

Manifestation is the process of attracting what it is that you seek or envision. In magical practices and in practices of self-care, manifestation is often at the root of our work. We all want something—more beauty, more peace, more time to create, more joy, more love.

For me, I've always visualized writing books in my manifestation work. I pictured myself writing something I loved and cared for, pulling whatever was in me out and putting it onto those pages, smelling that fresh-out-of-the-printer scent, seeing my name on the cover.

When visualizing, I pictured myself writing something beautiful that my younger self would love to read. I pictured writing words that could help people. I pictured writing poetry that captured the essence of who I am. I pictured making a dent on this earth by writing. I visualized the process itself: Opening my computer, typing on the keys, and pressing "send" to my hypothetical publisher.

What do you picture? What image has followed you throughout your life? Is there something, perhaps, that you manifested by sending it energy for years and years? What is the result, and what is the process by which you can achieve it? Close your eyes and picture it, swirling in shimmering, energetic light.

" *The universe is not outside of you.*
Look inside yourself; everything
that you want, you already are."

— RUMI

In many ways, the act of visualization is a conjuring in itself, but we can also ritualize our conjuring to heighten and nurture the manifestation process. Manifestation work can take many forms and shapes—from the highly ceremonial to the mundane. It can happen in one practice, or it can happen over a lifetime.

I like to think that the amount of time I spent sitting in libraries or up in trees reading or out at the park stapling fake books made of lined paper was my conjuring process. Later, I found that my vision had come true. I first self-published blogs and zines and books on my own, and then I made book deals with publishers. Our everyday, mundane actions are like water to the soil of our intentions.

With wordcraft, we use the inherent magic of creativity and language to call for that which we desire. We can use elements, archetypes, or just about anything else to do this as well. Put simply, you can use your journal to write your wishes, carve goals into candles, create sigils from letters, or create an altar with symbols and objects that inspire you.

Manifestation isn't reserved for those more spiritual or powerful or [insert stereotype]. We are all worthy of creating the life that we want, but we have to work within the realm of possibility, understanding that magic often brings to us what is already there, waiting for birth, seedlings deep in the ground. We are often asleep to our own potential, and in that discovery is a beautiful truth: If we trust the universe— and ourselves—we can make incredible things happen.

Manifestation is the converging of the occult and effort. Inner and exterior worlds collide in a dance of potential.

Our thoughts have bodies; they are real, breathing, and alive. Thoughts can transform into things, and the more we think on something, the more we can carve some of that thing into our lives.

Imagine your world as a tree. If you think hard enough on that thing that you seek—publishing a book, meeting new friends, building confidence—you begin to see it take shape, sprouting a small flower bed that grows into a lush garden.

It rises out from the wood, as indentations, ripples. It was always there. It was always possible. It was always within you. But it takes work and excavation to envision that thing as a possibility—to transform the idea of "doesn't exist" into "can exist"—to carve what we desire out of the wood.

The carving is the effect of both the imagination and the work we do to receive our desire. It's magic. But it's also, as we know, work. We cannot just expect something while making no inroads toward it.

And because manifestation is an excavation of self, we must prepare ourselves for that journey. It's both as simple as saying, "I want to write a book" and not even remotely that simple.

Manifestation: Knowing What We Can & Can't Control

I want you to think on something (or a few things) that you seek as we go forward in this chapter. Perhaps these are things that will happen within you: immaterial things, transformations, less fear, less rigidity, more receptivity to love. Or maybe these are more external things: a new job, the ability to travel, the drive or time to finish a project.

Journal on what these things might be and why you want them: What do they look like when you think of them? How do they fit into your life? What does it feel like in your body when you think of what you want—is it nervous excitement? Anxiety? A rush of warmth? Can you feel the water or the sun on your skin?

Now also think on what might be in the way of those things. Are there barriers you can control— like not doing the research or work of applying to a job? Or not having enough confidence to finish a project? Are you battling thoughts of "I'm not good enough"?

The good news: We can work through those internal barriers.

What about the external barriers? Is it time, money, or systemic disadvantage? It's important to recognize the barriers that you have control over versus the ones you do not. How does your dream then function within a tidal ocean that is constantly pulling you into its wake? What are the iterations of possibility?

When we talk about manifestation, we have a responsibility to talk about all of it. It's not just light and love and good vibrations, and anyone who says that is being reductive.

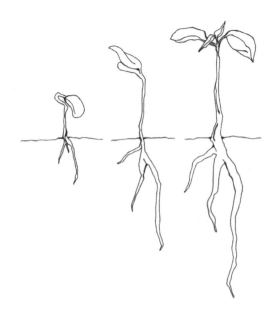

Some people say that if you just manifest hard enough, you can have anything you'd like. There are dangerous messages like this all over: If you have no doubt in your heart, you'll get what you want. Doubt, and you'll sabotage your own efforts. I don't buy it and I don't think that sort of thinking respects the depth of a magical practice or a person's soul.

Manifestation practices must be humanized and intersectional, just as witchcraft must be intersectional. We must be aware of our privilege and access. We must honor our doubts. We cannot pretend they're not there. We are not superhuman. We are people. We are witches. Our magic is a process, an exploration, a journey. There's no quick fix, no one-size-fits-all.

Put simply, it's easier to manifest more money and a higher salary and more vacation time when you're already at a place in your life where that is accessible to you.

It's important that we understand the way we talk about manifestation is going to be different across cultures and classes and people. For one, we cannot simply change the reality that longstanding issues around class, race, mental health, physical illness, and identity can slow or flat out prevent our access to the things we need.

And then there's us getting in the way of ourselves: Sometimes the things we think we want aren't really what we want at all. When we say we want to get married, do we mean that we want to feel safe or stable? When we say we want a lot of money, do we mean that we want to feel empowered in our careers, to have our basic needs met? To be able to care for our health?

Being aware of these many layers is key. You cannot truly engage with a manifestation practice without awareness.

In our wordcraft, we work through the layers of the self, honoring each one—the good and the bad. We write our way through the abyss. So, in these pages, you won't be judged for not "manifesting" hard enough.

You will never be told you are not deserving or that your vibes are not high enough. You won't be blamed for not being able to make something happen. And if you're thinking, "My vision isn't actualizing, so I must be sabotaging myself," stop. We've all been there, but we have to say no to those ideas.

In this chapter, we'll focus on manifestation of the personal and accessible—not tangible "things" or "items," but rather the impetus behind those things: self-love, confidence, receptivity.

We will conjure creativity and energy and create magical, conducive environments for manifestation. Of course, we'll be doing much of this on the page.

A Daily Intention & Manifestation Ritual

Throughout the darker months, it's helpful to think about healing the wounds, voids, and shadows of our lives. Darker, cooler seasons lead us to the great inner work.

By the time brighter months come along, the sun and energy wake us to the beauty of nature, reminding us that we can create the change we need. Sunnier seasons prompt us to shed our skin and inhabit the inner work we've done on ourselves. In this ritual, we will tap into that ebb and flow, our introspection and bloom.

Materials

A pen and paper
A large jar with a lid (or another
    container that speaks to you)

Each day, take a piece of paper and write two things on either side: In the morning, write your intention for the day ahead, and at night write on the other side what you worked on that day. This allows us to think of our growth and daily work goals as one. After you finish writing, drop the piece of paper into your jar.

Your intention (example: "I am making space for new creative projects") should be written in present tense. It can be for the tangible or the non-tangible. Your daily statement of work can be whatever you felt you did to contribute to yourself (example:

"I pulled a tarot card and meditated on what it means to go inward" or "I allowed myself to rest today.")

At the end of each season or on each solstice or equinox (depending on where you live and how the seasons play out), it may be helpful to look back and see the intentions and efforts you've made. Record these seasonal realizations in your grimoire poetica (see Chapter 6 for more on this).

> " *You are the storyteller of your own life, and you can create your own legend, or not.* "

— ISABEL ALLENDE

Writing the Self: A Moon-Phase Writing Practice for Telling Your Story

In this ritual, you will write the story of your life, bit by bit each day. Begin at the new moon and end at the start of the next new moon. You will find that a month-long writing practice helps to build your confidence with the ritual mindset while teaching you to find and honor your voice and story.

In this moon-phase writing practice, focus on releasing the old self and writing the new. Refer to a site or app (see Resources on page 172) that shows you the current moon phase and begin during the first day of the waning moon.

Materials

Cleansed hands
Your writing tools
Your sacred writing space
Clear quartz (optional)

Each day, in your sacred writing space, you may wish to keep a clear quartz near you. The clear quartz is known to aid in not only invocation and clarity of memory, but in protection and healing. The crystal can be held and caressed as a grounding object to bring you back to the present. If you feel lost or overwhelmed, hold the crystal and let it bring you back to where you are.

Before you begin writing, take several deep breaths. For about three to five minutes, breathe in and out slowly—inhaling for five seconds, exhaling for five. You may continue until you feel present and hyper-focused. This feeling is like a cocoon for your memory.

The goal is to write your life story in whatever way that feels authentic to you. Focus on the pivotal moments. Focus on the things that made you who are. You may want to focus on eras or decades, childhood, adolescence, adulthood. You may want to write about a single memory each night, from childhood up to today. Remember that this is about you capturing and honoring your essence.

Before you begin, decide what you'd like the outcome of your month-long moon phase practice to be. Do you want to honor your younger self? Do you want to pay tribute to your strength and bravery? Do you want to focus on writing through traumatic experiences with compassion? Do you want to let go of years of abuse or self-hatred? What is the narrative you want to rewrite or take back?

Begin with the beginning. Write as little or as much as you need. Who were you? What circumstances were you in? What was your first sense of pain? Of pleasure? What moments will you remember forever? What years or experiences shaped you? Write your goodbyes. Write your memories as things you no longer need to labor over. Write your light and hope and your small moments of victory and survival. As you come to the end of your journey, write of who you are today, how you are made of old shapes as well as new shapes. Be present; watch the shape of the letters as they carry your story out of you, taking the wound outside of you.

Explorations

Who will you become? What are you blooming into? What part of the person you are now comes from yesterday? End on what your story has taught you, and how you will carry its lessons into the future. Watch as the letters form; they are casting a spell. Your last line should be written in present tense (I am strong; I am free of guilt; I am softer than I was before; I am no longer running; I am here today; I am worthy; I am safe).

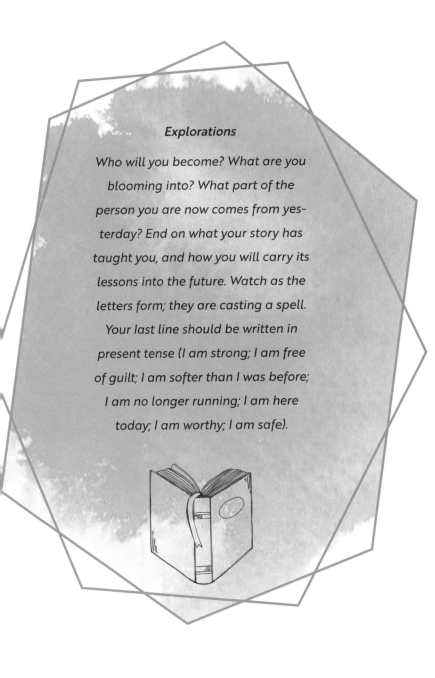

You Are the Magician:
A Tarot Writing Ritual

The Magician card as a luminous thing—beautified by bright colors, summoning the energy of creation and palpable generative magic. The Magician inhabits their own magic. The Magician not only summons and pools it, they direct it. This is a card of doing, of going, of creation, of channeling.

In The Wild Unknown deck (and in popular decks like the Rider-Waite-Smith), you see The Magician with the lemniscate symbol, the figure eight symbol that represents infinity, the interconnectedness of all things, and the self without limit. We are always connected to the infinite, drawing on it and being inhabited by it. Magic is a connection with that infinity—tapping into the wild greatness of nature and life and the cosmos. The Magician pulls on that energy, calls to it, finds an archetype of power and wisdom in it.

The Magician asks us to manifest our goals by understanding our vision and the drive behind it.

In this practice we will conjure our own power to get us used to feeling that electricity. To teach us to inhabit our magic. To lean into the infinite. Because any manifestation practice relies on our honoring that we are capable of all things.

Materials

The Magician tarot card

Items to represent the elements

A yellow candle (or a candle color that represents creativity to you)

Your journal

Scissors

A piece of cardstock or thick paper, like for painting

Colored markers and crayons in colors that invigorate and inspire you

---

Decorate your altar or space with things that empower you to manifest, conjure, and create: Use items that represent your power and magic.

Beautify with elemental symbols: crystals, a bowl of water, seashells, incense, feathers, a bell, a fan, soil, a flower, petals, salt, candle. Arrange the items with intention.

Invoking the unique energy of the elements helps to tap into the world around you. Take time to arrange this altar of creativity and manifestation. You are not small or separate from the universe. You are of it, and calling on it.

Light your yellow candle (a color associated with creativity) and meditate on it as you speak the following incantation out loud. (Better yet, I encourage you to write one for yourself).

I am infinite, of all things:
of air and fire,
wind and water, blood and starstuff.
I am full of and fillable, inhabited by
and inhabiting.
I am magic. I am potential.
I am conjuring and creating.

Next, journal on your intentions—for the next few days, the next few weeks, through to the end of the year. As The Magician, what do you call on? Focus on this with intent—just as The Magician focuses their energy. What are you called on to create, make, or be? How can you, in the short- and long-term, honor that?

Write a list of the what and the why, being specific, letting yourself be magnetized by potential. What do each of the elements teach you in your goals? To be more fluid, allow yourself to fly away? To have more energy? To be more grounded?

With your paper or cardstock, cut out the shape of the lemniscate. It's a simple figure eight, with two holes within each loop. Leave enough space so that you can write on it. Once you've cut this out, write your goals or mantras onto it—letting it carry your words into the infinite. Color it in with colors that feel powerful and brave and bold.

Seasonal Intentions: Using the Elements for Manifestation & Magic

The coming of each season brings with it all sorts of feelings. For the sake of being relevant to as many people as possible, we will focus on "sunny" weather—the part of the year where things bloom—and "cooler" weather—the part of the year where things go into hiding or die.

The colors, the flowers, the balmy winds, and the sparkling light of spring and summer remind us of life, potential, growth. In the cooler or darker months, we are reminded of the importance of going inward, reflecting, and working on the foundation of projects that will be born soon.

The seasons are complex. For many like me, the seasons permit us to sync up with nature, to climb into the greater flow. But let's be honest—the seasons can also trigger serious depressive feelings. It's important to connect with and recognize every one of those feelings. Magic isn't all light and love. Sometimes it's learning to make it through the night.

Write seasonal mantras for manifestation and intention:

I welcome the spring's golden light.

I am a new seedling each year, and with each spring I bloom again.

I feel my body mobilize, my mind sharpen, my heart soften.

I am the colors of newborn flowers. I am the color of rebirth.

As the animal kingdom sleeps, I permit myself rest and peace.

I find inspiration in the silent, bright, gray light.

I seek restoration as the snow falls.

As the leaves fall, I honor the cycle of change in nature and myself.

This season, I will create

_____ .

This season, I will become

_____ .

This season, I will grow

_____ .

This season, I will let go of

_____ .

Journal about the change of seasons and what they mean to you:

Everything changes form. We wilt. We bloom. And there's a certain comfort in knowing that we are flexible and fluid—that most of what we feel is temporary. The pain. The sorrow. The exhaustion.

When what we feel isn't temporary and can't be shaken off with the seasons, we can turn to the earth for a lesson in letting the light in: While we may have dark moments (or years), we can decide to unfold like a flower, to let the light nestle into our petals.

What happens when we let that light in just a bit? Can we find something to love or be appreciative for?

Turn to Nature Magic and Self-Care

According to the book *A Wilder Life* by Celestine Maddy and Abbye Churchill, there are many common herbs with a multitude of uses. Of course, use only with the permission of your doctor (to avoid contraindications or complications) and with regards to ethical and proper sourcing and usage. Many can be eaten, drunk in tea, ingested by tincture, or used as oils.

Some popular apothecary essentials:

DANDELION Anti-inflammatory and diuretic (eat or drink the tea)

GARLIC Antibacterial, can be used for cleansing wounds.

HOLY BASIL Provides renewal and energy; is considered an adaptogen, for helping the body handle stress.

SAINT JOHN'S WORT Mood-stabilizing, antiviral support, and can support the transition between seasons.

NETTLE May provide support for allergies and immunity.

PEPPERMINT This is a zesty kickstart for low energy, in addition to providing tummy support.

ECHINACEA This timeless remedy can help to prevent colds, infections, and support overall health.

GINGER This helps relieve nausea, gas, bloating, and other digestive issues

VALERIAN This is good for those seeking better sleep or a reduction in anxiety.

NOTE Please check with your doctor before using any of these herbs, as they are not safe for everyone.

Elemental Magic
A Spell-Poem for Inhabiting Your Wildness

The Uruguayan poet Marosa di Giorgio wrote of enchanted gardens—she grew up on a farm—where she encountered the liminal, death, nature, memory, and the body. There is a ghost flitting about in her words. In her work, this world and the otherworld collide as lilies and hydrangeas, and poisoned things hunt you down by night. Reality dissolves into something else. Di Giorgio, one of my favorite poets, writes poetry that feels inhabited by nature, speaking of and through it. It feels as though she is casting a spell to connect the human with the natural. She chews through the walls we build to make ourselves seem above or separate from nature.

Nature is our eternal guide, and spiritual practitioners and witches have always turned to nature for healing, messages, and lessons. The soul of the witch is made from fire and the sky and starstuff and sea and salt. It is this elemental honoring that enriches our lives and fuels our magic. When we call upon the elements in our craft, and when we represent the elements on our altar, we are asking the natural world to move the energy along, to hear our song.

Because in this book we will turn to the elements for inspiration frequently, we start here by inhabiting an element and letting it speak through you in a poem. First, select an element that speaks to you. Water magic has always been my go-to; it's where I feel at home. Which elemental language do you speak? You can learn more about the elements on page 64.

See what feels right. The goal isn't to pick a favorite. It's to spend time with an element, to conjure its power through the written word. You should come back to this ritual again and again, exploring your relationship to the different elements, and what each might help you learn and feel.

Materials

Cleansed hands
An altar space with decorations
    invoking an element (example:
    a candle, a cup of water, incense,
    or salt)
Your journal

Create an elemental altar (a small space on a shelf or desk at which you can focus and write); you may choose to do this at once or over time when you are ready to write this spell-poem. Collect items that correspond—either literally or metaphorically.

I connect with water, so I often decorate a shelf or part of a table with abalone shells, pearls, vials of sand, a bowl of water, a cup of tea, and photos of the pebbly Italian beach where I once felt sheer ecstasy. You can use household items, too, like a cup of water or a tray with an ice cube. Never, ever be afraid of using the basics; many witches do!

Once you've decorated your altar, take several deep breaths and close your eyes. Envision the element you're working with, and feel the power emanating off the objects around you.

Begin writing a short poem that calls on the element. This should be kept short, as you'll use it as an invocation in your practice should you ever need that element's energy. You'll want to start with, "Water, I ask you" or "Fire, I ask you," etc. Be unapologetic, creative, metaphorical, and wild in your language. My version, a spell asking the water to grant me adaptability and willingness to experience depth, is below:

Water, know my name.
Be of my body. Bring me into the
depths of self.
Water, I ask you to cleanse me of my rigidity, to speak
in languages of change and movement.
I ask you
to create in me a shore. To create
in me a sea. Between the worlds I move,
blood of changing tides.

COLOR MAGIC

According to Sarah Potter, witch and color magic practitioner, color magic embraces the color spectrum, as well as the inherent energy of each color, in our magical workings.

Potter recommends using certain colors for certain intentions, which I have listed below. Get creative with your color choices!

Feel free to use a crayon, marker, pen, or even paint. Use these colors with intentionality while writing or creating sigils, but also in altar decoration (think flower petals, fabrics, and candles). Beyond black or blue, which are the colors of most pens, think about using:

Orange: This bright, optimistic color invokes inspiration, luring the muse from its sleep. Use this when you're writing spells, poetry, or manifestations—especially around generative or creative endeavors.

Purple: This rich, nourishing color helps you develop intuition, just as an amethyst crystal may invoke your psychic spirit. Use this color to call on deeper truths and wellsprings of creativity.

Green: This natural, fertile, earthy color calls for abundance of all sorts, material or otherwise.

Red: Use this carnal, fleshy color to invoke desire and pleasure—and to do sex magic.

> " *The words emerge from her body without her realizing it. as if she were being visited by the memory of a language long forsaken.*"

— MARGUERITE DURAS

Conjuring Creativity: List-Making Practices for Writing Goals & Inspiration

Many readers of this book may not identify as writers by trade. Some are, of course, but others simply love to write for themselves and in their magical practices.

If you want to work on any sort of writing project—or if you simply want to get your creativity flowing as a magical energy—this is a foundational illumination practice I use to conjure the lifeblood of my writing.

It can be used for a specific project or it can be used for general creative momentum. It's not a magical practice per se, but it does engage your energy and cast your intention into the universe. List-making also helps to settle the turbine of thoughts that precede any work. It slows you down, gets you to focus, and helps you call on yourself

Materials

Journal
Citrine (optional)

———————————

As you write, keep a citrine on your desk. Hold it, place it on your page as you write, or simply carry it with you on days you need a creative boost. Citrine's bright, sunny color is known for stimulating energy, drive, creativity, and self-growth. Interestingly, citrine comes from amethyst—its oxidation causes the difference in color. This crystal is a literal symbol of transformation, of taking one thing (inspiration) and turning it into another (creative output).

> **Practice 1:** In your journal, make a list of words or phrases that describe how you want to feel after you have completed or begun a writing project. How can this project transform? How can working on your writing magic change your life? How can it help you speak your truth? By doing this, your words are conjuring your future reality.

Some words and phrases that come to mind for me are: Freeing. Destigmatizing. Empowering. Validating. Creatively fulfilling.

> **Practice 2:** Make a list of descriptive words that conjure the mood of your writing project (or what you'd like to gain from a new wordcraft practice).

If I'm working on a set of poems, say, set on the beach, that invoke a feeling of freedom and watery energy, I'll include: *Golden. Watery. Luscious. Verdant. Bright. Hazy. Dreamy. Expansive. Horizon. Luminous. Blooming.* Hang these words up on your altar, paint them into artwork, carve them into candles with corresponding colors ("luminous" might be written on a yellow candle, while "blooming" may be written on a green candle). Write them on tiny scrolls and bury them in your purse or wallet; carry their energy with you so they can inhabit you and you can inhabit them.

Practice 3: List objects that inspire you in your writing and creative practice. This could be a list of objects you have or some you may want to add to your collection—for your altar, for use during ritual, or just to have in your space to inspire you.

These might be crystals, plants, books, special writing pens, photographs, incense, candles, or a velvet golden throw blanket. Begin to find the objects—household and mundane objects work, too—and sprinkle them into your space. Taking the time to envision your space helps you tap into your powers of intention. Creating a magical space is a spell in itself.

" *Everything in the world began with a yes.*"

— CLARICE LIPSECTOR •

The Sacred & The Mundane:
Spelling Your Intention

In the 2018 remake of Suspiria by Luca Guadagnino (original Suspiria enthusiasts, please do not hate me) the main protagonist, Susie, moves from small-town Ohio to 1977 Berlin to dance with a renowned dance troupe at the Markos Dance Academy slash witch coven. From scenes of her childhood, we see Susie obsessively drawing a disorganized map, scribbling dozens of black directional lines from America to Germany, willing it to be. Whether this was her fate or not, she was actively taking part in the fulfillment of her dreams, using her energy and focus to conjure this unconscious need.

And, as we learn, Susie wanted to dance. She wanted to dance so badly she, without proper training, memorized the dance "Volk," which she would perform for the Academy.

She snuck away to see the school's performance and was punished for it. It didn't matter. She wanted this. Eventually she conjured herself the leading role in "Volk"—although there is much, much more to the story than that. One way that she did this was by creating a map for herself, using her hands to draw the literal path she would follow.

But as we see, Susie's manifestation of her vision had both an occult component and a work component. She followed up on her vision by putting her time, effort, and energy into actualizing it.

When we speak to the Universe, we have to keep a promise to it: If you—beautiful, wild world—part the way for my vision, I vow to, from earth, do the same.

A practice that has become sacred to me reflects Susie's compulsion for mapping her way to Berlin. Often, when I feel directionless or need to make my vision concrete, I map it. In this practice, you'll do the same— but you'll add candle magic to up the ante.

Materials

Your journal
A large sheet of paper
A marker in a color that inspires you
Several small votive candles (with
    candle holders, trays, or another
    safety object)

_____

First, create a sigil for manifestation
(see page 58 on sigil creation). In
your journal, create one from a word
of your choice—a word that aligns
with what you need to actualize your
vision. Perhaps it's drive, practice,
resourcefulness, focus, creativity,
discipline, or something else.

Next, use a large sheet of paper to
write out, in the center, your ultimate
goal. Be specific. Write in the present
tense: *I complete a book.* As vines
stemming from the center, draw small
bubbles to contain the actionable
things you can do to power your goal.
Write these in the present tense:
*I wake up earlier. I am disciplined.
I meditate before writing.*

Once you've finished this, set a votive
beside each actionable thing. As you
go, intentionally light each candle, one
by one, drawing the sigil beside each
actionable item. Speak each out loud,
letting the flame ignite your will.

Finally, draw the sigil around your
main goal. As your hands move, be
mindful. Envision the energy of the
sigil, powering your intention. Speak
this intention several times out loud.
Paying close attention to how the
sounds carry your will into infinity.
Into the place beyond you, where
thoughts become real.

As you work through this practice, be
mindful of the work that you must do
to nourish your goal. Manifestation
is something we do without noticing
we're doing it (by daydreaming, for
example)—but it's also something
we do in an intentional, dedicated
ritual setting.

An important note: Do this somewhere safe and be sure to watch over
the candles; let the candles burn until
they go out.

Manifesting Change at the Community Level

A s a magic-maker or witch, your practice is intimately tied to nature. And with this connection comes a sacred bond: a promise to care for your community and your planet. We are all natural beings, and being divorced from this mentality does not serve us. It keeps us disconnected, lonely, and fighting for our lives and the lives of species across the globe.

While "manifesting" is often thought of as a magical practice, its roots are in the mundane: Once we think of doing something, we put our energy into making it happen. Magic simply helps us ritualize that process.

Work with other witches or your coven to make changes at the community level.

You don't need a coven to manifest change, but if you have the privilege of working alongside other witches (even digitally), you can come together to focus on change. Plenty of witches have come together to bind evil-doing politicians or cast spells for greater good, and you can, too. Find a small group of witches or magic-making friends to brainstorm about community issues (just stay safe).

Some ideas:

- Work together to gather clothes or create a clothing drive to support the local homeless shelter. Charge the clothes beforehand so that they find the right home and deliver joy and peace to the person who wears them.

- Join a community garden to do volunteer work; as you plant seedlings and tend to the earth, speak with it. Send it love and gratitude.

- Join a community grief group as a volunteer (these are often held at hospitals or churches).

- Bake cookies or other goods and charge them with healing intentions. Give them out at local events or markets.

- Get a group of friends together to write spell-poems for a zine; have the proceeds go to a charity that supports a marginalized community.

- Draw a daily tarot card and interpret it as a hopeful message; share that message on your social media account as a way of supporting others and sharing wisdom.

- Write a letter of support to your community and publish it with your local newsletter. Gather names to sign off on the letter.

- Shop at locally owned businesses—especially those run by marginalized people—and use your words to write beautiful reviews of their items on social media. As you publish these words, set an intention of support for the business. When you work alongside others to donate your time, speak out using whatever platform you have, or use your words to write letters to your local government agencies, you are casting a spell.

Small actions lead to big changes, and while these moves may not be explicitly magical, there is magic in combining energy to support the greater good. Witches have long been looked at and reduced to malicious characters who boil children and poison crops, but the fact is that witches have also been the people who take part in social justice initiatives. In New York City, spaces like Catland Books host readings and events that fight against sexism or racism or explore the intersection between social justice and magic. When we speak out, especially in unison, we make change. What could be more magical than a gathering of voices creating change from nothing more than their own demanding words?

Using Social Media to Set Intentions & Send Support to Others

On *Luna Luna's* Instagram account, I posted a beautiful image of the sea. I'd taken the photo off the coast of Italy on my travels and always looked at that trip as a sort of intention-paid-off adventure. I'd set an intention to go and made it happen. In the caption I wrote, "Let's cast a spell together: Tell us a short-term goal you have—be it finishing a book or simply getting more rest. By commenting below you are casting your intent. 'Like' and reply to others to add a little extra magic."

As a response to the status, people shared their intention, ritualizing it by commenting and casting their wish into the world. But the most beautiful thing was that people wanted to help support others, sending a little witchy "like" as if to say, "I've got you."

When we acknowledge one another's wishes, we build compassion into our everyday lives. Even if someone comes from a completely different place you can meet somewhere, even briefly, to say, "I honor your needs and desires."

Magic isn't just self-serving; it's an opportunity to water your own garden in hopes that you can pass it forward. A witch fights for abundance and peace beyond themselves.

Explorations

Write your own manifestation spell for a short-term goal. Think on what you can manifest in your life and the impact it will have on you and on others. What power do you have to make it happen? How can you become more receptive? What sort of shadows are you dealing with through it—and can you address those in your spell work? What actions can you take to throw open the proverbial curtain and let the potential in like luminous light?

CHAPTER 5
MINDFULNESS MAGIC

Rituals and Writing
Prompts for Developing
Presentness, Intuition,
and Receptivity

You are standing on a cliff, high above the sea.
Hundreds of tiered buildings adorn the hillside,
rooftops shimmering in the sunlight. There
are clouds above you, moving quickly as if to
make space for the next batch to pass overhead.
Below, alleyways twist and turn, with staircases
descending directly into the water. You look out to
the west, and see fuchsia flowers hanging from pots
in the distance. To the east, you can see another
continent—or is it an island?—far out beyond the
horizon. There is something there that wants to be
seen and known. The scent of something moves
through the air. There are stairs to your right. You
descend, moving through time, into an ancient
village speckled by ruins. But you think nothing of
the past. You stay here, in your body. You think only
of now. If you could capture the here and now, what
would you say? What are the words that live within
you when you are in a space of total freedom and
beauty? What words do the clouds form when you
let yourself see past their shape? What do you notice
when you let yourself coil into the stillness of it all?

Capturing the Moment

Consider the Roman city of Pompeii, eternally preserved by Mount Vesuvius's 79 CE eruption. Through its ancient streets, we see the handwriting on the wall: Images and phrases, etched in walls of homes and taverns—notes from one person to another.

Often times these statements were general or political. And sometimes you'd find words written on the insides of people's homes that roughly translate to phrases like, "I had a great time dancing with you."

Now, thousands of years later, we can walk through that same energy—the infinite pulsing of human connectivity.

We look to poetry and paintings as preservations of humanity, but the graffiti or symbols painted on walls tell a different story, one that isn't institutionalized or commissioned by the powers that be. There's a greater truth there, something messy and raw and human.

If you wrote a message to your future self, or to humanity, what would it say, and how would you say it?

Even more so, what is it in the moment that you'd want to proclaim? What is so special and beautiful that it should be preserved? In this very moment, what mundane thing are you feeling, doing, being?

So much of magic and art and creativity is about capturing the details—the essence of the here and now, the light and the sound, the scent and the space. It's about learning to inhabit the present. It's about being comfortable right here, right now, so that you can escape the call of sorrowful nostalgia or the need to plan the future down to the minute.

What are the things you notice when you step outside of the rushed, habitual, onto-the-next-thing mindset many of us adapt? What happens when we slow down to ponder the slow, soft

process of seasons? Of sunrise into nightfall, of the gentle unfurling of flowers. Of the tide, which is in no hurry at all, and of the constellations, which move according to their own path, undeterred by expectations of going-going-going. We are always moving, and yet, in that, when we stop just to be, there is a magic that happens.

Mindfulness is the act of being present and embracing the transcendent mundaneness of being alive.

Being a witch is about being in tune with the everyday magic of things. Of making morning coffee. Of watching the herbs grow. In mindfulness, we see the way the light falls. The way the clouds move, heavy and dark. The way breath feels as it moves through the body. It is at the very core of magic.

The writer is a mindful creature. Whether you're writing a story or a poem or a letter for healing, the best way to infuse your wordcraft with magic is to be mindful as you write, noticing all the little details that you feel and are and desire.

Without seeing, it is hard to create. Because of this, mindfulness is the foundation of the magical lifestyle. Without it, how could you notice anything? How could you truly tap into the essence of self?

"*I'm aware of the mystery around us, so I write about coincidences, premonitions, emotions, dreams, the power of nature, magic.*"

— ISABEL ALLENDE

Recognizing & Translating Intuition

What does intuition feel like? If, in an attempt to explain intuition, we write what it feels like—how would it read? Would intuition appear as sounds? Would intuition read as words or phrases or images or colors?

And, when we talk about intuition, what do we really mean? Is it the realizing of something, the absolute knowing of a thing, without evidence or knowledge of any kind? Our gut is usually tuned in to what's around us—and yet we often ignore it. It happens every single day. This is because it's hard to always be paying attention, always living in that liminal state, and because we've been told throughout the years that intuition is unprovable, weird, wacky, and false. We live in a time of numbers and figures that make no space for the invisible.

But these premonitions and flashes of information can help us in the mundane world: Who seems untrustworthy? Does that slightly off feeling require a doctor's visit? Should we check in on a friend who has gone silent? Is someone acting strangely or are we being "too sensitive"? The truth is right there, in our palms, waiting to be seen.

In your *grimoire poetica* (see chapter 6), keep a tab of these premonitions, insights, and clairvoyant messages. On the left hand side of the page, describe the "knowledge" and on the right, describe the sensations associated with this knowledge. It might reveal that an image of a person is related to anxiety, fear, or danger. Or perhaps you had a job interview and felt a flash of "this won't end well." These feelings are worth noting, as the more we record them, the more we start to realize the patterns and synchronicities—all of them asking to be understood. The witch is as powerful as her deep knowledge; this deep, dark, watery underworld of knowing can be a source of wisdom and protection throughout your life.

FULL MOON MEDITATIVE MAGIC

Meditation has always helped us peer inward, past the noise. It helps us seek wisdom from a higher self, or from a divine source, and it doesn't need to be difficult.

When we meditate, we become mindful of our needs and feelings. We can recognize them, honor them, and let them pass on by. We can embrace the calm of simply being.

In mindful magic, we meditate by sitting still, following our breath, and seeking an altered state. In this place, feel your body as an entity of energy, alight in shimmering colors. What color pours forth from and into you? What does that color mean to you? On each full moon, enter into a meditative state. This grounds and centers us—ready to be imbued with the cyclical and natural power of the full moon. In this ritual, we learn to reflect, reset, take back control, and seek power under the light of that rich, shimmering moon.

Once you are mindful of your feelings and emotions, let them move through you. Don't try to steer or question them. Simply let them be. Breathe into them.

As you begin to wiggle out of this state, awaken and journal about your experiences. At this stage, you are more aware, more malleable, more willing to think on what you feel. Only now can you question and think on it, whereas in your meditative state, you learn to let it be.

We draw our deep magical powers—compassion, intuition, knowledge—from these quiet, meditative moments. What are you aware of when you listen in?

" These, our bodies, possessed
by light."

RICHARD SIKEN

Movement Mindfulness: The Sacred Dance

According to the sixteenth century Southern Italian myth of the dance of the tarantula, a woman by the name of Anna Palazzo was bitten by a tarantula and, feeling on the verge of death, she frenetically, ecstatically danced until she was cured. "As she dances, she becomes the spider that bit her," according to the Italian anthropologist Ernesto de Martino in his book *The Land of Remorse: A Study of Southern Italian Tarantism*. But tarantism is more than just a response to a spider bite; it is a ritual of excavation and suffering from the pain and grief of life.

The magic of dance is global. Even before Anna Palazzo's story, a kind of ecstatic dance was found in ancient Greece, where people trance-danced in worship of Dionysus, the god of wine and ritual and ecstasy. In ancient Egypt, dance was used in sacred rituals. The practitioners of voodoo use dance to be inhabited by Spirit. And the list goes on.

In *Witches All: A Treasury from Past Editions of The Witches' Almanac* we read, "Hardly a phase of occult history is without reference to the use of dance as a means of entry into a mystical state for the purpose of worship, divination, or gathering power from the atmosphere itself."

Witches dancing around a bonfire—it's a vision we've seen time and again. You can dance under the sun to attain its energy and vigor; you can dance under the moon to call upon its powers of insight and intuition, moving your body as the sea, tides rolling in and out. Dancing is a way of raising energy.

It doesn't matter if you've never danced, are a professional dancer, or use only half of your body to dance. Dance is a direct connection to the higher self—and

" I move, therefore I am."

———— HARUKI MURAKAMI

perhaps even the spirit world. It is a communication with our cells, a celebration of our sensuality, ferocity, and spontaneity. You can dance with your hands, your whole body, or your hair. You can dance seated in your room or outside while the sun sets in a garden.

Mindful dancing is the practice of letting yourself go into the ecstatic: noticing your blood pumping, remaining aware of your bones and muscles, listening to your breathing, feeling your heart pump.

You can use your body to conjure messages from your environment; do you feel joy, hope, strength? Do you feel tenderness, patience for yourself, energy? Write it as you move, or after a dance session.

You can also create a sigil and dance its shape into the air around you, embodying your magic. Sketch your sigil onto paper and memorize its shape or spontaneously create sigils out of dance. Breathe in with

each stroke, and breathe out on the next, inhabiting the creation of the sigil. Breathing life into it. Using your arms to trace it into the sky, or circling your hips into the shape of the sigil. Letting yourself move freely.

And, like the tarantula dancers of the past—and today, as the dance is still performed—we can exorcise our demons through dance. How can you dance your wounds away? How can you use your body to tell the story of your pain? Can you dance until you sweat, finally arriving at the emptiness of thought and the full presence of the body?

Did you feel free? Clumsy? Did it bring up a specific feeling for you? Did it "click"? Did you feel exorcised of a feeling? Fear, worry, doubt? Did you inhabit your body? Journal about how it made you feel. Try to translate the feeling of the body onto the page.

POETRY OF THE HERE AND NOW

When we write mindfully, we train our minds to focus and intuit and raise energy. This develops our magical workings and helps us become more creative spell writers.

- At your local park, settle in and watch the grass sway. Watch the birds and squirrels come and go. What do you see? What conversations is nature having with your body? Journal it.

- Find a color near you. Try to understand it. Translate it. Be there with that color, within the moment. What is the color transmitting? How does it change the space? What does it feel like, or sound like? What is saffron? What is blue? How does it fill the room? Write it.

- Before bed, capture your mood in a poem. Is it frustration? Anxiety? Fulfillment? How does it feel in your chest, in your throat, in your bones, in your gut?

- Light a single candle and stare into its flame, breathing deeply. What is it that the flame is doing? Focus on it as you free-write. No edits. No censorship.

- Get yourself into a trance state with deep breathing. Write what comes to mind; build a poem around this when you are fully conscious.

- Dab on some perfume. What does the fragrance do to you? What emotion does it evoke? Write it.

> " *It's possible to understand the world from studying a leaf.* "

JOY HARJO

Feeling Flames: Mindfulness & Compassion Toward Others

According to a study by the American Psychological Association, how we treat ourselves is directly correlated to how we treat others. This means that when we are compassionately mindful of ourselves, we begin to treat others with the same compassion, patience, and kindness.

Mindfulness practice means sitting silently with the self and letting thoughts pass by un-judged. It means meditating and experiencing feeling without being overpowered by reaction. It means being mindful about how we feel toward others. Finally, having a mindful magical practice means getting honest with yourself.

When we are angry with someone, frustrated by them, or sad for others, we don't often get to show them. This is especially true for relatives or friends with whom you might have a complicated relationship. The urge is to care for them, but often we cannot. Or the urge is to snap at them and let them fucking have it. Sometimes we can't do this either.

When we are mindful of our feelings, we can be more mindful about why others are the way they are. Mindfulness teaches us to make space for whatever it is we feel and at least be willing to see others with compassion.

Of course, not everyone deserves our love, respect, compassion, and patience. Sometimes people are vampires; sometimes they bleed us dry.

Because of this, we want to manage the way they make us feel. In this case, you'll want to write statements onto small pieces of paper to be ritually burned.

I am patient with my mother, even though I feel frustrated.

My friend is acting out of hurt, and I have compassion for that, even though it affects me.

I am drawing boundaries with my father and that is okay. I can still support him in ways that work for me.

I am full of rage but hopeful that I can transmute these feelings into forgiveness.

Read your statements out loud and then burn them in a fire-proof bowl (please do this near a sink, if possible). As you finish reading the statements, burn them. This not only gets rid of the evidence, it uses the energy of the fire to empower your intentions. Ask out loud to be filled with compassion, acceptance, or forgiveness.

Explorations

Write a spell for intuition. Call on any guides, archetypes, ancestors, or symbols of intuition, asking to be open to insights and wisdom. What would your spell look like if you integrated mindfulness into it? How can mindfulness help us tap into that deep, all-knowing inner well?

DAY OF SILENCE

The brain loves silence. It craves it. According to a study in the scientific journal Heart, just two moments of silence can nourish the brain in a profound way, reducing stress and creating space for healing. In our hyper-connected world, we are constantly surrounded by noise, music, traffic, and the ever-streaming river of stuff that we deal with on a daily basis.

In this practice, you'll spend a day in silence, disconnected in as many ways as possible, reducing text messages, conversations, and even music. Fill in the spaces that you would typically fill with music or distraction.

From sun up to sun down, if and when possible, keep quiet. Investigate, listen, explore. Tap into yourself and the world around you. Listen to the water trickle in the fountain. Listen to the birds. Refrain from speaking (unless completely necessary). What emotions arise? What begs to be said? What felt important, but becomes less so? Are you lonely? Are you in need of human contact? Do you find that silence has nourished you? Does your intuition increase? Do you feel more connected to nature? How does it feel?

In silence, we become mindful, deliberate, sacred. When we clear all mental clutter, we make space for authenticity and vision.

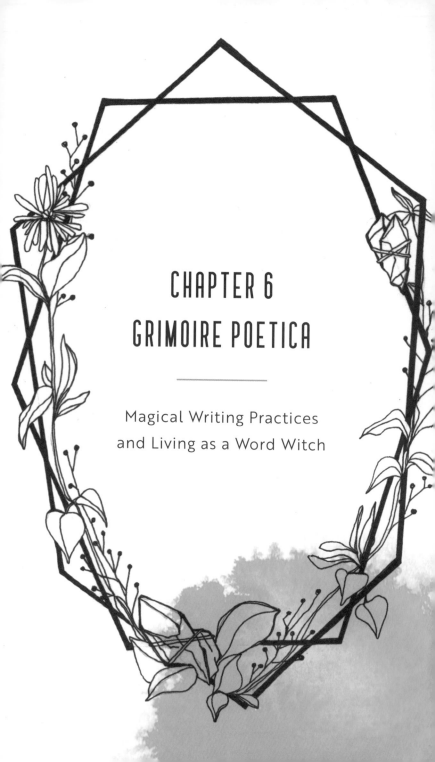

CHAPTER 6
GRIMOIRE POETICA

Magical Writing Practices
and Living as a Word Witch

From dream recording to astrological poetry, this chapter is about exploring more open-ended ways to write magically. These exercises and ideas may be stored in your grimoire, or *grimoire poetica*, as I call it. It's a creative, poetic, less structured collection of your magical workings and creative writings, part magical-recipe collection, part literary exploration of you: It's a sacred book of self.

The term "grimoire" is sometimes used interchangeably with "Book of Shadows," though there are slight differences. A Book of Shadows, for many witches, is a diary of personal magical workings. What worked? What didn't? A grimoire is often a book of magical notes—on which herbs to use for what, candle colors, or crystals. I tend to call it a "magical journal" or grimoire, simply because that resonates with me. Many witches and magical practitioners collapse these types of books into one another.

And for many of us who use magical writing, words encompass our magic. This means our poems are spells and our automatic writings are explorations of self. Our journal entries are a magical act of sacred self-mining, and our stories or letters to the dead are ritual acts. So, in our grimoires, process and result can be one and the same.

Therefore, we can turn to our *grimoire poetica* as a place to write spells, poems, journal entries, and notes to ourselves about our magical processes, in addition to notes on ingredients or spell timings. Should you want to divide these into separate journals or books, please do! This should feel intuitive and easy for you.

Unlike previous chapters, you won't find specific kinds of ritual here; rather, you'll find additional open-ended ideas for filling your grimoire pages, as well as prompts for further self-exploration. I encourage you to find what calls out to you. You can also refer to this chapter as you work through the rest of the book.

Astrology as Self-Reflection: Writing Horoscope Poems

According to *Astrology in Ancient Rome: Poetry, Prophecy and Power* by David Wray, there was once a time when astrology wasn't just an interest but a government function. As Wray writes, "Divination or prophecy through reading the signs and portents of the sky was not merely a folk belief in the ancient Mediterranean; it was also part of the state religion at Rome. There was a group of official priests known as augurs whose functions included reading omens in the sky."

While things aren't exactly the same today, the long-time intersection between art and astrology continues: From Marcus Manilius' *Astronomica*, a poem focused on Hellenistic astrology, to Western astrology's influence on poetics (see social media accounts like the Astro Poets, written by Dorothea Lasky and Alex Dimitrov), it is clear that art and the heavens live in the same glorious mansion of mystery and deep humanity.

There's a reason so many people flock to astrological memes and apps and accounts. For one, more and more of us are turning inward and looking to the metaphysical and the natural world for answers, autonomy, and insight. The cosmos provide an opportunity for us to search inward and question our role in the world, even if we use the signs as archetypes that prompt self-reflection.

More and more of us are focusing on self-healing, self-reflection, self-growth, and magical systems of thinking—especially as racism, sexism, and classism run rampant. When we meditate on these cosmic archetypes, we focus on the layers of the self—allowing ourselves to disconnect from the

constant din of digital chaos and tap into something ancient and potent and thought-provoking.

Reading your horoscope daily is not the opportunity to say "that's true!" or "that isn't true!" but the opportunity to explore the magic of peering inward, of diving off the cliff of sense and obviousness. In reading a well-written horoscope, we often think, "How does this fit into what I know to be true?" But perhaps the question should be, "How does this prompt me to explore parts of myself that I haven't even considered yet?"

Not every horoscope is going to apply to everyone, as there are simply too many variables at play. But once you decide to ask yourself, "How can I find myself here? Where are the parts of myself that can respond, in some way, to this?" you can begin to unravel the liminal—finding yourself the center of a burning star.

As Anaïs Nin says, "we don't see things as they are, we see them as we are." When we write poetry, we write through the lens of the self. And when we read our horoscopes, the same thing happens. There is always room in both a poem or in a horoscope to play and reframe and think. The answer is that there is no answer. You get to decide what it means for you.

A poem can be a talisman, an artifact of the self, a metaphor in a language that we must decode.

The stars, in all their infinite light and distance, help us get closer to unraveling our own mysteries and illuminating the shadows of the self. The constellations, the heavens, the position of the stars during your time of birth—these things are asking you to let go of what you can see and know and prove and touch, to look up into the sky—up into the headier parts of yourself—and conjure your secrets and fears and loves.

Is that not poetry in itself?

When you read your daily horoscope, write a poem based off of it—not just what it says but what it makes you feel, worry about, realize, or hope for. In this practice, you will commune with the stars, a kind of transcendent magic that changes lives.

" If we want a real spirit to settle into our words, we can present them with care, art, and magic."

——— THOMAS MOORE, *THE RE-ENCHANTMENT OF EVERYDAY LIFE*

Bibliomancy: Literary Divination

Books speak to us, create worlds for us, and conjure both the questions and the answers that reside within us. When we turn to books and written texts for some greater message, a message from beyond the page, we become bibliomancers. Bibliomancy (which goes by many other names) is the use of books in acts of divination. The goal here is to find greater wisdom, to lean into that Force or Spirit beyond and yet within the page.

Like the ancient practice of *sortes*, the practice of divination from drawing a card or other object, bibliomancy has long had a place across cultures and in many folk traditions. Bibliomancers traditionally used the Bible for divination, although grimoires and other sacred texts were also used.

According to the University of Michigan's Romance Languages and Literatures, poetry—how delicious!—was consulted as well. The *Dīvān of Ḥāfeẓ*, a collection of ghazals written by the great Persian poet Hafiz, was used to seek "Tongue of the Unseen," or messages via the poet after his death. Today, it's still common for people to use sacred texts, like the *I-Ching* or the Bible to divine wisdom.

When we use poetry, of course, there is a technical term for that: *Rhapsodomancy*. However, bibliomancy seems to cover it for most people.

Like tarot or astrology, bibliomancy asks us to lean into the mystery and examine what we've been told. What is revealed? What does this revelation ask of us? What sings out when we see the words before us?

In this practice, you'll open a book—whatever book calls out to you. As a poet, I prefer poetry. If you'd like, you can ask a guide or spirit to direct you to passage. Then, with eyes closed, select a

> " What can be explained
> is not poetry. "

— W.B. YEATS

page and a line. From there, the given line can be taken as wisdom, an omen, or a sign. Intuit this. Sometimes, people place the book on its spine and let it fall open. Although there are many approaches to bibliomancy, it is best that you create your own approach.

Now you try it: Let a book fall open and let your instincts guide your finger to a page and a phrase. Investigate what the line could mean in the context of your life.

What images does it bring to mind? How does it make you feel? What does it force you to think about that perhaps you had not before?

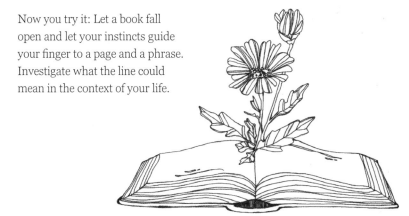

Sprung from the Self:
Poetry as Spellcraft

In 2017, I wrote a piece, "Poems are spells," for the magazine *Venefica*, which was published by the wonderful Catland Books in Brooklyn, New York. I've long explored the idea of poetry as occult work. In my latest book, *Nympholepsy*, I wrote poems as a sort of eulogy to the past. The book was a binding— of people, of an era, of a self I no longer carried within me.

As a Scorpio, poetry is my way of shedding skin. Poetry is rebirth. For you, a poem may be a way to encapsulate, honor, and bind a time of darkness. A poem may even be a hex (you'll find no hex-hate here; to each their own).

As witches, we carry a great energy inside of us. Unlike people who don't spend time directing or manipulating that energy, we are always aware of it. This is an incredible thing—it allows us to be free; to find relief, purpose, and clarity. Poets do this too; we create an altar on the page, we pull together our tools and objects and we move toward a sense of finality. And just like witches, we poets love our rituals: wine, a cigarette, a cleansed space to work, a quieting.

Each word, meticulously selected as an ingredient or power object. Each section, a turning point, an incantation, a taking-out to the crossroads. Each turn of phrase, a candle lit by the wick of another. And when read out loud, all at once, it is a ritual, a spell cast.

When we write poetry, we are using energy in a specific way: while writing a poem, we program it with our intention. Is it a poem of personal power? Of memory? Of reclamation? Like an incantation or a mantra, we can read a poem any time to evoke the energy we programmed into it. It will always be there, encapsulated in the moment we created it. It can transport us, infuse us, remind us.

There's magic in choosing likeness, simile, metaphor, the in-between of words and meaning and reality: So much of magic is about associations, about the power of deciding what we want something to mean. A rose may symbolize love; water might symbolize fluidity—in poetry you decide your associations. You might build an entire grimoire in your poetic practice by deciding that the word sea means death.

If you build your spells out of poems, you get to live inside the microcosm that you've created, where your language and vision is the ultimate force. You get to flex your magic muscles, straddle a world where a thing is a thing but is also not.

I once wrote a poem about a pale, white horse on fire, in a sort of dreamscape where my ancestors sprung up from the ground to put the flames out. For a long time, I read that poem to crowds, and no one knew the horse was me. I was asking to be saved. And every time I read it, I called on them to save me. The poem changed me as I read it. Eventually, I stopped reading that poem, and I stopped reading the book I wrote it in (it was called *Andalucia*). Some part of me felt that I'd been saved, that it was time to move on, that I'd been heard. In that intimate setting, I'd spoken my demands and they'd been heard.

It was the process of reading it that had changed me. This poem was my spell; it was my token. It was a canvas for the future me to spring from.

In your grimoire, write your finalized poem-spells. Some ideas:

- A poem-spell to conjure a message in your dreams

- A poem-spell to honor the beauty and limitations of your body

- A poem-spell to call upon your ancestors

- A poem-spell to confess your deepest secret

- A poem-spell to purge your greatest fear

- A poem-spell to summon your inner power

- A poem-spell written in a magical alphabet

- A poem-spell about a person or place that haunts you

Poetic Conjuring: Poem Prompts for Witches

Poetry moves and slides and breaks rules. It defies structural convention. It says, "I won't tell you the truth, but I'll tell you a part of it." It gives you clues. It asks you to think. It reveals according to its own rules. That's why we ask, "But what is it about?" And that mystery is why it's so beautiful—both to read and to write. It helps us stretch our imaginations, get out of our comfort zones, and it offers a glimpse of something that one might never see or realize or pay attention to, begging for you see it through your own lens. As a poet and a teacher of poetry, I think that is fucking magical!

WRITE THE LIMINAL Write a poem that speaks of the in-between, the crossroads. What does it look like at dusk? What does it feel like to be almost touched, almost loved, almost lost? How do you capture what it feels like to straddle the liminal in a poem?

WORD WORSHIP A book of poetic spells, *The Lost Words* by Robert Macfarlane, aimed to reclaim and celebrate natural words that were taken out of the Oxford Junior Dictionary. These words—acorn, adder, bluebell, dandelion, fern, heron, otter, and willow—were replaced with words like blog, broadband, bullet-point, cut-and-paste, and voicemail.

What words mean something to you? What words speak to your memories and personal power? Are there words that speak to your identity, your resistance, your body, your journey? Choose five of these words and write a five-stanza poem using each of them, or write five poems (as a set, to be read out loud together) using each.

DREAM POETRY When we wake up, our minds are loose and fluid, capable of magic—still tethered to other conscious states. The moment you open your eyes, tap into your dream space and write a poem about your dream. Let its contradictions and messiness and weirdness soak into your poetry. What is the dream's message? Write that message into your poem. In this way, you are divining from the subconscious mind, mining the dreamscape, and channeling it from the ether into a physical thing to be explored and tapped

into. Dedicate a whole section of your grimoire to dream poetry and you'll watch the themes and messages unravel—allowing you to swim in a literary sea of the self.

HERBAL POETICS Are you a fan of cannabis or mugwort? Both are used for spiritual purposes, opening a sort of mental portal. In a high state, write what comes to mind. Don't bother making sense or trying to define meaning right away; just let your feelings guide you. Ride the wave of the self, and let your words slip onto paper, unregulated. Light your joint with the flame from a candle lit in your sacred space.

You can read more about weed witchcraft at *Luna Luna*, www. lunalunamagazine.com. Just search for *Weed Witchcraft: A Ritual with the High Priestess of Smoke*. In it, Moxie McMurder writes, "Smoking the holy herb is a spiritual act, one that puts you in touch with the four elements and when practiced correctly can lift the veil and reveal and nature's secrets." Just remember to stay safe, be legal, and talk to a doctor before using any psychoactive substance.

Flora Poetica
Asking Nature for Messages

According to Cheralyn Darcey, flowers speak to us—of healing and creativity, love and intention. But because the language of flowers is so mysterious, we must learn to translate it largely with our intuition.

This language has long fascinated humans. During the Victorian era, flowers and plants were used often as tools of communication, called floriography—although it is also referred to as floramancy. Petals and colors contained the power of a message, and combinations of flowers told a story.

This technique developed mostly because Victorian etiquette didn't always allow for open communication—especially of complicated thoughts or desires. In 1879, Miss Corruthers of Inverness published a book exploring flower meanings called Le Language de Fleursand. *In her words, receiving a gardenia meant to have secret love. An oleander? Caution.*

" *I paint flowers so they will not die.*"

——— FRIDA KAHLO

Of course, for our purposes, we won't be following a guide. Instead, we'll be communicating with the flowers themselves, and writing from the experience. In green witchcraft, this communication is common and a beautiful way to let the earth move through your conscious and unconscious experience.

New flowers whisper of life and rebirth. A tree of two hundred years has witnessed so much; what does it know of pain? What can it tell of resilience?

In this practice, we'll turn to nature—the starstuff, the soil, the greenery, the bare trees of winter, the scent of rosemary, the marigolds in the pot—both to heal our bodies and to find peace.

This idea of the healing power of nature has been researched by credible scientific journals, such as the Journal of Inflammation Research, *which have found a link between earthing—spending time, feet to earth, in nature—and its positive effects on our health. Forest bathing or earthing can boost endorphins, reduce inflammation, regulate heart pace, and reduce cortisol. After all, the earth has always been our healer, long-prized by cultures who understand the language of the land.*

Materials

A local park, a trail, a beach, a small
    rooftop garden, or even a part of
    your home with plants
A journal

———————

While in nature, communicate with a
flower (or plant or tree) of your choice.
Be sure not to trespass, pluck, or walk
on protected or fertilized ground. You
should also ask every living thing if
you can work with it before you do
(and be sure to say thank you!).

Ask it to guide you through your
feelings: Ask it about your grief; ask
it about your wounds. Ask it about
your creative goals. Ask it to tell you
something you don't know. As you sit,
preferably skin to earth, ask your little
flower to guide you through the pain.
Write down whatever comes to mind.
Imagine a cord from the root of the
earth connecting to a flower or a tree,
pouring through it and into you. What
message do you receive? How are you
connected to the earth?

When we translate nature, it may
be imperfect. It may be in words or
fragments, ideas or concepts. It may
be in colors or emotions. A tree may
sing, "gratitude" while a flower might
say, "You have no choice but to
be reborn."

But what of difficult messages? Even
if you don't agree with something
that you're sensing, channeling, or
intuiting, write it anyway—often,
these "I don't agree with this"
moments are worth a deeper dive.
Like people, nature has a dark side.
What is hiding beneath the surface?

Perhaps it asks you to see a truth
you have not allowed yourself to see.
Perhaps it asks if a part of you is dying,
thirsty, dirtied, sick, mutated, toxified?

*What are you being asked
to confront?*

What is it that is hiding, masked?

What is juxtaposed?

Write it into your grimoire, and be
sure to describe the tree, plant, or
flower you are working with.

Come back again and again. See
if you can develop relationships
with these natural beings. Are lilies
always willing to nurture you while
the oak tree begs for deeper shadow
work? Dedicate pages in your journal
to each of these species and the
communications you have with them.

If you grow your own flowers, you
may want to pluck them and press
them into your journal or grimoire to
keep them forever. Immortalize and
honor their wisdom in this way.

Hypnos: Dream Rituals & Diary-Keeping

Throughout almost every culture, dream interpretation is a powerful divining tool. When we learn to recall and interpret our dreams, we develop an understanding of self that gives us a sense of autonomy and lucidity around our hopes, desires, wounds, and traumas—all of which play out in vivid color in our dreamscapes.

The ancient Greeks believed that pre-sleeping rituals—bathing or refraining from eating fish or meat—would lead to specific kinds of dreams. They would sometimes sacrifice an animal for a god whom they wished to visit in sleep. Hypnos, the Greek god of sleep, was the son of darkness (Erebus) and night (Nyx). Hypnos lived in the underworld, full of poppies and plants capable of lulling you into a soft, dark slumber. Through the underworld ran the river Lethe (forgetfulness). This intersection invokes that liminal state between awake and asleep, where we risk forever forgetting what we have just dreamt.

Often what we dream is disturbing; other times, it's beautiful. Often our dreams are incoherent, messy, hazy—requiring us to decipher as best we can. When we begin to pay attention to the themes and the emotions with which we wake, we can better understand ourselves. As witches, our self-understanding is a crucial part of developing our magic, writing the spells that we need, and finding the path toward personal empowerment. And when we understand ourselves, we can better help others as well.

Upon waking, immediately write down or record into your grimoire poetica your dreams, notating:

- Colors
- Weather
- Themes (rushing, being lost, exploration, abandonment, dance)
- Mood or tones
- Rooms or places
- Emotions within the dream
- People, archetypes, or figures
- Dreams within dreams or memories
- Recurrent dreams (are they the same, or slightly different?)
- Powers or lack thereof
- How you feel upon waking up

If you're having nightmares or insomnia caused by bad dreams, create a nighttime ritual. According to the journal of the *American Academy of Psychoanalysis and Dynamic Psychiatry*, patients with chronic PTSD benefited from establishing rituals—just as the Greeks did— to work through nightmares. Patients saw in later dreams that these rituals worked.

What kind of ritual you create depends on your needs. Here are some ideas:

- **Create an altar dedicated to Hypnos:** Figures of the moon or stars (or even cut-outs from a piece of paper), a piece of valerian root (valerian is used to induce sleepiness), a sachet of lavender (used to relax the mind), amethyst (believed to promote dreaming and intuition), a candle, and perhaps a poem dedicated to Hypnos, asking for sleep and positive dreams. Anything you don't have on hand you can draw or write out onto a piece of paper. Remember that words invoke as objects do.

- **Create a nighttime playlist:** Curate it with soothing music, chosen to evoke a specific emotion before bedtime. Listen while slowly stretching, bathing, or simply moon-bathing. This may not be magical, but music can change an environment and evoke a mental state.

- **Sleep with a protective crystal:** I like to sleep with a rose quartz under my pillow, a crystal that has long been used as a symbol of love and protection, encasing me in a field of soft love and care. Charge your rose quartz, or whatever crystal you prefer, by moonlight before use, as the moonlit energy will lull your body into a peaceful sleep. These associations can be powerful tools for the mind.

- **Write what you'd like to dream about:** Use your words to describe the kind of peaceful slumber you hope to have; what are the feelings, colors, sensations? How much sleep do you want to get? Write it in the affirmative: "I get seven hours of sleep, dreaming of beautiful things, like islands and flowers. I am at peace in sleep. Sleep restores my body and my mental health."

- **Write a pre-sleep poem-spell to be read out loud at your bedside or under the covers:** Light a single candle to initiate bedtime. Here is mine, which you can use—though I (of course!) encourage you to write one for yourself.

I become the dark garden between
then and now,
suspended in the twine of Hypnos;
body soft and cradled of ivy. In this flora I am the earth.
I am the darkness
beneath it. And the darkness beneath that. I am the
purest sleep. I am pure primordial quiet. I am tended to
by the stars, alight and shimmering, protected.
I am the golden
hour of the body, saying goodnight to the day.

"Freedom of expression is the foundation of human rights. the source of humanity and the mother of truth."

— LIU XIAOBO

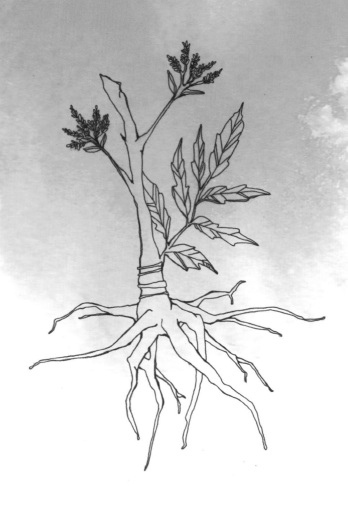

THE MAGICAL WRITING GRIMOIRE

Using Social Media as a Word Witch

While your practice is ultimately private, part of being a word witch is using wordcraft responsibly. This means understanding that your words have value, power, and roots; a word can creep into the soil of society and grow—as a poison plant or as a healing flower.

In today's largely digital and hyper-connected world, we turn to social media as a way to connect, tell our stories, and honor the stories of others.

When we see people post statuses like, "I'm having a bad day. Send good thoughts," this is a sort of modern grievance ritual. Like wearing all black to mourn, this is a digital veil—a public ritual asking for support and love. In this way, the words—and even the emojis—have great power.

But words can be dangerous, too. This is why we cannot tolerate hateful, racist, sexist, or other shameful words. Bullies uttering words of hate can drive people to self-harm. Politicians, community leaders, celebrities, editors (and anyone in even a semi-public position of influence) can click "post" or tweet a sentiment of hate, exclusivity, and prejudice and instantly create a ripple effect in society. People internalize these words, words which can often demean and poison a culture. People say "words can never hurt me," but this just isn't true.

It's up to us to hold wordcraft as sacred and to use our words responsibly. Spreading words of support, inclusivity, and vulnerability—to your network, in letters to politicians, in letters to the editor—matters. "But I only have 300 followers!" you might say. But if a million compassionate, empathic people have 300 followers, that's a reach of 300 million. When words of love are spread en masse, the energy field shifts.

Suddenly, those words permit others to live, to embrace self-worth, and to trust in others.

When Maya Angelou sat down to speak with George Stroumboulopoulos in 2014, she said the words, "Tell the truth, to yourself first—and to the children." In her words, we are reminded of the scope of her power as a writer and civil rights activist. By speaking her own truth, she permitted countless others to explore theirs. To speak out. To sing.

In our sharing on social media, we can remain private and still be impactful. You can share stories of the self, of course, but you can also share ways to support marginalized people, people who need assistance, or ideas for stepping up in your community.

We can share stories that reveal our vulnerability and truth, in an effort to make others feel less alone. We can use specific words to underscore the importance of a matter. I often use my Instagram to support foster youth, the chronically ill, marginalized voices, and people with PTSD. In every post, I ask myself what my words can accomplish. I ask myself what I can contribute.

We can write mindfully and magically by sending healing thoughts and energy into our words and watching the words as they take shape on the screen or paper.

We can say a mantra as we publish our posts, sending the message out with intention to find the right reader. We don't have to view social media as a waste of time or energy; it can be a tool for magic and beauty and goodness. And when we do this, we lead by example, changing the very fabric of the digital world. Our words are seedlings that will grow into a hundred flowers.

Writing has been perceived as a high art, only for those lucky enough to get published. With social media, it is democratized. We can all reach people today. We can all use our platform to spread change. And if that's not magic, what is?

The Witch in the Mirror

When you look in the mirror, do you see a witch? What sort of witch do you see? A healer? An empathic leader? A seer with the wisdom of ancient myth? A sensual lover? A kitchen alchemist?

And when you look at the witch in media, cinema, and literature, do you see yourself?

The question is: Can we find ourselves in the witch's autonomy, self-reflection, hunger, and creation? In the vulnerable pool of self? Do we find the witch when we resist norms? When we resist oppression?

What happens if we expand upon the witch? What happens when we become our own archetype? You are permitted to become the multilayered, diverse, wildly unknowable, previously undefined witch you want to be. You are permitted to transcend existing archetypes and write your own narrative into existence.

We all want a more empowering and inclusive world for ourselves and for others, where we are free to bloom safely. We are all moving away from being told what to do and moving toward

what we can do for ourselves. And in that move toward freedom we recognize the evolution of language and its meaning.

You may invent your own alphabet, your own language. Maybe you discard the word "witch" and invent your own word for your magic. Maybe you blow it all up and create your own direction, requiring no permission and giving no apologies. Maybe you are the oracle.

Find what resonates with you and write it. Write it into being. Write your name and your demands. Write your vision and your story. Rewrite your story and be born again. Write what's dead and burn it. Cast it. Cast it out. Conjure it. Within you, there exists a mirror for truth, a salve for the wound, a lantern in the fog.

The process of exploring your inner magic is non-linear, liminal, imperfect, authentic to you alone, and creative. Embrace this, and you will discover the richness of life that you deserve. Your words can conjure something beautiful and wild and free—for yourself, and for the communities you inhabit.

Sharing Your Magic & Wordcraft

Many of us keep our magic private, but should you want to share your poetry, stories, or magical process ideas with others, let's create a word witch community together. Use the hashtag #MagicalWritingGrimoire #WordWitch. I would love to read your words and creations. Please follow me at @lisamariebasile and at @Ritual_Poetica for writing prompts and more from my *grimoire poetica.*

Using Your Voice and Power to Support Others

After reading this book, I encourage you to continue using your voice to speak up for others, especially those who can't speak up for themselves. Every word you speak or write—on social media, in letters to your local government figures, and in texts to your friends—has power. To that end, while we may be reading and utilizing this book, there are many people, especially in marginalized communities, who do not have the privilege of reading or writing. It is up to us to use our power to fight for them. Please consider searching sites like The Charity Navigator to find global and local organizations that fight for widespread access to books, that help to improve literacy rates, and bring the power of writing to groups that need it.

Resources

Books & Magazines

Light Magic for Dark Times
by Lisa Marie Basile

Nympholepsy by Lisa Marie Basile &
Alyssa Morhardt-Goldstein

*Moon Magic: Your Complete Guide
to Harnessing the Mystical Energy of
the Moon* by Diane Ahlquist

*Sigil Witchery: A Witch's Guide to
Crafting Magick Symbols* by Laura
Tempest Zakroff

Tarot for Troubled Times by Shaheen
Miro and Theresa Reed

*Intuitive Witchcraft: How to Use
Intuition to Elevate Your Craft*
by Astrea Taylor

The Collected Poems of W.B. Yeats
by W.B. Yeats

Ascend Ascend by Janaka Stucky

*Women Who Run with the Wolves:
Myths and Stories of the Wild Woman
Archetype* by Clarissa Pinkola Estés

*Magical Alphabets: The Secrets and
Significance of Ancient Scripts*
by Nigel Pennick

Sex, Lies, and Handwriting
by Michelle Dresbold with
James Kwalwasser

*The Art of Death: Writing the Final
Story* by Edwidge Danticat

*The Literary Witches Oracle: A 70-
Card Deck and Guidebook* by Taisia
Kitaiskaia and Katy Horan

A Wilder Life by Celestine Maddy and
Abbye Churchill

*A Little Bit of Astrology: An
Introduction to the Zodiac*
by Colin Bedell

Witchery: Embrace the Witch Within
by Juliet Diaz

Waking the Witch by Pam Grossman

*Witches, Sluts, Feminists: Conjuring
the Sex Positive* by Kristen J. Sollee

Venefica Magazine edited by
Melissa Jayne

Apps

Sanctuary World
www.sanctuaryworld.co

MOON
www.charliedeets.com/moon

Mystic Mondays
www.mysticmondays.com

Tarot Decks

The Wild Unknown Tarot

The Wild Unknown Archetypes

Rider-Waite-Smith Tarot

Websites

Luna Luna Magazine
www.lunalunamagazine.com

Bibliomancy Oracle
www.bibliomancyoracle.tumblr.com

The Hoodwitch
www.thehoodwitch.com

*A more comprehensive list of
resources, texts cited, inspirations,
and further reading ideas can be
found at www.lisamariebasile.com/
magical-writing*

About the Author

Lisa Marie Basile is the founding creative director of *Luna Luna Magazine*, a popular magazine and digital community focused on literature, magical living, and identity. She is the author of several books of poetry, as well as *Light Magic for Dark Times*, a modern collection of inspired rituals and daily practices. She's written for or has been featured in *The New York Times*, *Refinery 29*, *Self*, *Chakrubs*, *Marie Claire*, *Narratively*, *Catapult*, *Sabat Magazine*, *Bust*, *HelloGiggles*, *Best American Experimental Writing*, *Best American Poetry*, *Grimoire Magazine*, and more. She's an editor at the poetry site *Little Infinite* as well as the co-host of *Astrolushes*, a podcast that conversationally explores astrology, ritual, pop culture, and literature. Lisa Marie has taught writing and ritual workshops at Manhattanville College, Pace University, and HausWitch in Salem, Massachusetts. She is also a chronic illness advocate, keeping columns at several chronic illness patient websites. She earned a master's degree in writing from The New School and studied literature and psychology as an undergraduate at Pace University.

Follow her at @lisamariebasile and @Ritual_Poetica. Follow *Luna Luna Magazine* at @lunalunamag.

Acknowledgments

This book is dedicated to all writers and poets who write their truth, to the witches and magic makers who fight for change and beauty, and to those who have, despite obstacles and trauma, conjured transformation in their own way.

Thank you to my team at Fair Winds Press/Quarto—Jill, Meredith, and Anne, and to my former editor, Jess. Thank you to my friends (you know who you are, and I love you) and family—especially David, mom, and dad—for allowing me to write my own truth. Thank you to Benjamin for your tireless inspiration and support. It is not always easy to love a writer.

But mostly, thank you to those people who generously read, review, edit, feature, and share my work and find light in my words.

Thank you for reading this book.

Index